Classic Cooking Made Easy

Classic Cooking Made Easy

C.P. Fischer
M. Piepenbrock
Barbara Rias-Bucher

CLASSIC COOKING MADE EASY

A Cookbook and Videotape Program

BARRON'S

Woodbury, New York · London · Toronto · Sydney

First English-Language edition published 1985 by Barron's Educational Series, Inc.

Copyright © 1984 by Grafe und Unzer GmbH, Munich, West Germany

The title of the German edition is *Fantastisch Kochen Leicht Gemacht.*

All inquiries should be addressed to:
Barron's Educational Series, Inc.
113 Crossways Park Drive
Woodbury, New York 11797

Library of Congress No. 85–7438

International Standard Book No. 0–8120–5663–9

Library of Congress Cataloging in Publication Data

Fischer, C. P.
  Classic cooking made easy.

  Translation of: Fantastisch kochen leicht gemacht.
  Includes index.
  1. Cookery, International. I. Piepenbrock, Mechthild.
  II. Rias-Bucher, Barbara. III. Title.
TX725.A1F53713 1985 641.5 85–7438
ISBN 0–8120–5663–9

Printed in Hong Kong

5678 490 987654321

Preface

CLASSIC COOKING MADE EASY: That's the idea behind this new kind of cookbook. It is meant for everyone who not only loves to *eat* well, but wants to be able to *cook* well.

The desire to be not just an adequate but a truly good cook has never been simple to fulfill. Too often there are gaps in an aspiring cook's basic knowledge of ingredients and techniques, and to perfect cooking abilities he or she needs expert and comprehensive instruction. That's what this book is for: It shows you, in the simplest terms possible, how to be a fantastic cook by clearly illustrating all the important techniques and explaining each step in detail.

This book has as its goal to present recipes in as basic and understandable a manner as possible. It shows you how to cook step by step, in text and photos. Nothing is left to chance; we show you how each step should proceed and how the finished dish should look. The photographs clarify any tricky procedures; they will give the experienced cook more confidence, and even the beginner is assured of success if he or she follows them precisely. You will see, for example, the expert way to marinate a large roast, how to quick-cool custard in a water bath, and the techniques for preparing a feather-light cake roll. Clear, detailed pictures are enormously helpful in complementing written directions; text and photos work together to give you a cook's instinct for the right sauce or batter consistency or how to gauge the exact doneness of a roast. The pictures also illustrate the little tricks that are so important to a cook's success: You will see how best to peel and seed tomatoes, clean bell peppers, prepare and stuff poultry. The beautiful result of each recipe is shown in a color photo that is a treat in itself.

As for the detailed text, even experienced cooks will find tips for making the job easier and more foolproof. Any difficult steps are explained with special care, and the reasons for doing things one way and not another are spelled out. Of course, it's always more satisfying to understand why you should proceed in a particular way than simply to follow instructions by rote.

We have structured this book according to classic menu order, so you will find chapters on soups and one-pot meals; salads and first courses; and fish, meat and poultry dishes. There are further chapters on egg dishes, vegetables, and side dishes, and not least is the varied assortment of desserts.

American readers will find classic European specialties and techniques—a superb marrow ball soup, a pork roast that's guaranteed to be juicy inside, crisp and crusty outside. You will see how to make inexpensive meats like ground beef and veal shoulder into elegant entrees. Or take chicken: No doubt you've had chicken curry before, but if you haven't prepared it with a homemade spice mixture you have no idea what you're missing. All the spices are available in well-stocked supermarkets, specialty shops or health-food stores, and the small extra effort of mixing them yourself is amply repaid by exquisite flavor.

No doubt you've also had a simple potato gratin or scalloped potatoes, but try adding leeks to the dish—and you'll find it a lot better. Try also a gratin of kohlrabi, fennel or apples (the latter a marvelous accompaniment to pork or game); all three recipes are included as variations on the basic Potato-Leek Gratin. To save space the variations have been written in briefer form, but their preparation is so similar to that of the master recipe that lengthy explanation is unnecessary.

Likewise for Braised Beef Rolls: The classic stuffing consists of onions, bacon and pickles, but we also offer an unusual variation using feta cheese, pistachios and currants—not to mention Veal Birds, another variation on the roulade theme, this time stuffed with hard-cooked eggs.

With the help of this book, then, you will find a surprisingly wide range of foolproof recipes at your fingertips. Try the basic *spaetzle* recipe once; you'll soon find yourself proceeding to spinach, herb or liver *spaetzle*, and from there on the experimentation is up to you.

We've also included recipes for some classic French, Italian and Greek dishes. You'll find *Lasagne al Forno*, *Saltimbocca alla Romana* and the famous *Ratatouille* of Provence. We could go on at length listing more Mediterranean specialties—and a few Oriental ones as well—but your best bet is to leaf through the book and see them for yourself.

As far as ingredients are concerned, they are limited to items that are readily available in any supermarket or, as the case may be, at your butcher, fishmonger or greengrocer. The recipes use common ingredients dressed, as it were, in new clothes. We also took pains to make the recipes reasonably thrifty to cook; food need not be expensive to be delicious.

And since everyone who cares about food wants to know more about it in addition to simply eating it, we've peppered the recipes with interesting information—sometimes about the ingredients, sometimes about the origin of the dish and so on. A calorie count is given for each recipe, and there is always an approximate preparation time to help you plan ahead. Any lengthy interval of marinating, chilling or the like is also noted so that you will know ahead of time to allow for it. And nearly every recipe concludes with suggestions for suitable accompaniments.

At the end of the book is a menu collection that will help you in planning the perfect meal for any occasion—formal or informal, with family or guests. You will find suggestions here for hearty, stick-to-the-ribs meals, light summer party menus, and just about everything in between. The preparation time given in each recipe is a great help to menu planning as well, since it will enable you to prepare the meal in a logical sequence, to cook ahead of time where practical, and to avoid last-minute fuss.

Finally, CLASSIC COOKING MADE EASY has one more special thing to offer: the chance to supplement your knowledge of cooking with a 60-minute home video cassette that shows the complete preparation of all the dishes marked with the symbol. With this videotape you'll see on your own TV screen how a leg of lamb is prepared, cooked and carved; how a chicken is stuffed and roasted; how chocolate mousse is made. Naturally this is the best way to demonstrate how a dish is prepared, for after you've seen it a few times on film, you'll know the recipe so well that you will feel as though you've made it yourself. Thus forearmed you can return to the kitchen to try out your new knowledge at the stove.

We wish you happy cooking, and we have no doubts about the culinary successes you will achieve with your family and friends.

Contents

This symbol indicates that the recipe is included on the videotape cassette. If you are using this book in conjunction with the tape cassette, you'll want to follow along in the book as you view the tape.

A Word About Equipment

Whoever likes to eat—and to cook—well must have the proper equipment. Selecting it is not easy, considering the vast array of cooking paraphernalia available in department stores and housewares shops, because not everything that's good-looking or heavily promoted will prove to be as useful as anticipated. Here's a word or two of advice to help you choose what you really need.

A logical place to begin is with pots and pans. The best pans conduct heat well, are sturdy and are easy to clean. The most prized saucepans are made of copper, which is usually the choice of professional chefs. Copper is the best heat conductor—that is, it heats up quickly and evenly.

Copper pots are unfortunately very expensive. The purchase will be worthwhile, though, if you make sure before buying that you're getting good quality. It's important that the bottom and sides of the pan be equally thick; if the sides are too thin they are likely to overheat and give the food a scorched taste. Be especially wary of copper pots sold at prices that seem too good to be true. For these bargains in particular—though of course the same is true of all copper vessels—be sure that the inside is fully tinned. Food should never be prepared in a copper pan that is not lined with tin; use such a pan strictly for decoration.

You will probably do best to buy copper pots in a cookware shop whose management is knowledgeable enough to guide you to the proper quality and where you can be confident that the pots will be of sound design, with sturdy handles and tight-fitting lids.

Good pieces of copperware deserve careful treatment. Always use wooden, not metal, spoons and spatulas against the tin lining, and never use abrasive cleaners. Whenever possible, soak the inside of the pan with hot water and dishwashing liquid while the pan is still warm, so that food will wash away without scrubbing. Stubborn, crusted-on bits will loosen if you add water to the pot and bring it to a boil.

Stainless steel is another superior cookware material; moreover, it's easy to care for. In some cases stainless does a better job than copper: green vegetables and homemade noodles, for example, retain their fresh color best in stainless steel. Here too, of course, you will get the best value if you buy the best quality. Look for pans with a thick bottom—preferably with a copper and aluminum core—and equally thick sides; the lid should fit well and the handle must be fastened securely. Some stainless steel pots are sold with a steamer rack that fits inside.

Like copper pots, stainless should be washed only with grease-dissolving detergents, not with abrasives that will damage the surface.

Enameled cast iron also makes fine cookware, as the metal is an excellent heat conductor. These pots and pans can be used both on top of the stove and in the oven, and they are easy to care for. Like any other pan, cast iron should have a smooth, perfectly flat bottom and a tight-fitting lid. The enamel coating makes this equipment easy to clean, but the same caution applies as for other cookware materials—though the enamel is tough, it can still be damaged by abrasives or metal implements.

Aluminum is a very good, extremely fast heat conductor that warms food quickly. Aluminum pots are good for cooking large quantities of food because the pots themselves are lightweight. But remember that a heavy bottom is still important to prevent burning.

Next come vessels of glass, earthenware, stoneware and so on, which with a few exceptions are just for oven use. Fortunately it is well known by now that the glazes must be lead-free. If you have any hand-thrown or ethnic pottery that you're not sure of, use it only for decoration or for serving such things as fruit or nuts.

Aside from saucepans, skillets are also a necessity; here again there is a multitude of choices. The heaviest materials are best:

copper, stainless steel and cast iron heat quickly and evenly to seal the surfaces of fried or sautéed foods. Thin, lightweight skillets will warp and dent so that they do not lie flat on the heating element and consequently do not heat evenly. Skillets coated with a nonstick material are excellent for foods that are to be cooked in little fat and at moderate temperatures. Alongside the cookware itself, knives constitute an equally important category of cooking tools. Though they're on the expensive side, you simply cannot stint on good knives. The knife must fit correctly in your hand, with the blade in proper proportion to the handle and the latter neither too thin nor too short. The weight is also important. Too light a knife will not sit securely in your grip and will undoubtedly be made of inferior steel. High-quality blades possess different elasticities depending on the knife's function: chopping knives and cleavers need a very hard, rigid blade, while a filleting or boning knife must be somewhat flexible. To keep blades well honed use a sharpening steel from time to time—ideally, before each use. Knives should always be washed by hand in hot water, never in the dishwasher.

As a cutting surface use a stable wooden board, not metal or any such very hard material. After every use scrub the cutting board with detergent and a brush under hot running water; stand it vertically to dry to minimize warping. You will also need a carving board and meat fork for roast. The fork is more for holding the meat down than for lifting it up, because piercing roasted meat with a fork will only let valuable juices escape.

Naturally, kitchen spoons should not be lacking; choose between wood and plastic. Flat wooden spatulas are particulary useful for stirring soups and sauces as they cook. You should also have at least two wire whisks—a light, flexible and fairly large one for whipping cream and egg whites, as well as a stiffer, heavier one for folding and blending. Both should be made of stainless steel; it is rustproof and hygenic, and it will not discolor foods or lend a metallic taste.

Ladles and skimmers should also be made of stainless steel—they will be easy to clean and will not take on food odors. Likewise bowls, colanders, strainers. Good utensils should, insofar as possible, be made of one piece of metal, without rivets or welds. Superior equipment may seem expensive at first blush, but its initial cost will be more than repaid by its long life and versatility.

A very useful piece of equipment, and too often overlooked in American kitchens, is the conical strainer. It has several advantages over ordinary round sieves. The food being puréed or strained goes exactly where you want it to, so that a sauce can, for example, be strained out of a large skillet into a small bowl without running down the sides. Moreover, if you have a pointed strainer made of stainless steel, leftover cooked vegetables and such can be pressed through without causing the metal to bend out of shape.

Finally, let us not forget the little gadgets that make cooking more pleasant and efficient—melon ballers, vegetable peelers, apple corers, lemon zesters, crinkle cutters. . . . The melon baller can also be used to cut carrots, celery root or potatoes, which will look attractive and absorb more flavor during cooking because of their greater surface area. Citrus fruit makes a lovely garnish when scored with a zester. These specialized knives and blades aren't absolutely necessary in every kitchen, but once you have used them you'll not want to give them up.

Marrow Ball Soup

This must be cooked at a gentle simmer; do not boil.

1 pound boiling beef, such as tongue or short ribs
2 large marrow bones, to yield about 2 ounces marrow
1½ quarts (about) cold water
1 onion
8 black peppercorns
2 whole cloves
1 garlic clove
½ bay leaf
1 bunch soup greens
1 small parsley root
1 bunch parsley
2 to 3 sprigs thyme
1 tomato, coarsely chopped
2 teaspoons butter
1 egg
1 egg yolk
⅔ to ¾ cup fine dry breadcrumbs
Salt
Freshly grated nutmeg

4 servings
360 calories per serving
Preparation time: about 4 hours
Cooling time: about 2 hours

Rinse the meat—it is not necessary to dry it — and place in a large saucepan.

- Push marrow out of bones and let stand in cold water until you are ready to prepare marrow balls. Rinse bones and add to meat in saucepan. Add cold water to cover. Bring to simmer, uncovered, over low heat.
- Halve the unpeeled onion. Place an ungreased heavy skillet over high heat until very hot. Add onion halves, cut sides down and brown thoroughly; the onion will give the soup its golden yellow color.
- Add onion halves to meat mixture with peppercorns, cloves, peeled garlic clove and bay leaf and simmer gently, un-

covered, for 2 hours, replenishing water as necessary. The soup must only simmer; that is, small bubbles will rise to the surface.
- Skim foam as it accumulates, if you wish; it is not absolutely necessary, however, as it will eventually settle to bottom of saucepan.
- Meanwhile, trim and wash soup greens; shred or thinly slice parsley root. Rinse parsley and thyme and shake off excess moisture.

- Tie together soup greens, parsley root, about a quarter of the parsley, and thyme. Add to soup with tomato and simmer 1 hour longer.
- Remove meat from saucepan and reserve for another use (it can be used for stews).

- Pour broth through conical strainer lined with muslin or several layers of cheesecloth to remove whole spices, vegetables and particles clouding the broth.
- Let broth cool; if time permits, chill for easier fat removal.
- While broth cools, prepare marrow balls. Blot marrow dry, chop finely and melt in small skillet over very low heat. Transfer melted fat and remaining bits of

marrow to fine strainer, pressing gently on solids. Let marrow cool.
- Mince remaining parsley.

- Add butter to marrow and blend until creamy. Add whole egg and yolk and beat again until creamy. Stir in breadcrumbs. Season with salt, nutmeg and about 1 tablespoon chopped parsley. Let mixture rest 30 minutes.

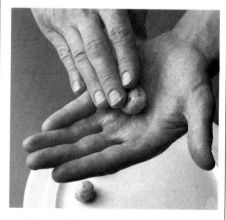

- Pinch off hazelnut-size pieces of marrow mixture and roll into balls between the palms of your hands. The marrow balls should be smooth and without cracks, or they may fall apart during cooking.
- Degrease broth. Pour some of broth into saucepan and bring to simmer. Add marrow balls and cook gently for 20 minutes, partially covered; do not let broth boil.
- Heat remaining broth over moderately high heat. Season with salt and remaining parsley.
- Add marrow balls to soup and serve very hot.

For many discriminating diners a good soup is the most important component of the entire meal. You can cook a large quantity, divide it into portions and freeze it, so the soup is ready to serve on a moment's notice. This recipe can be used as the basis for many other soups. For chicken broth, for example, use a large stewing hen (about 4 pounds) and substitute white peppercorns for black. You can also make a broth using only soup bones: Instead of the meat, use about 1 ¾ pounds of meaty bones. Blanch them briefly in boiling water before adding to the soup to prevent cloudiness.

Potato Soup with Bacon

Be sure to use mealy potatoes, such as russets, for this exquisitely creamy soup; the potatoes should fall apart in cooking. The soup tastes best when made with a strong broth of beef, bones and vegetables, but in a pinch you can substitute canned broth or even instant bouillon.

A wonderfully warming soup for cold days.

1 pound soup bones

1 marrow bone

2 quarts cold water

1 pound boiling beef

Salt

1½ pounds baking potatoes

7 to 8 ounces carrots

7 to 8 ounces celery root

1 leek

1 parsley root

Small handful of celery leaves, chopped

1 bunch parsley, chopped

5 ounces bacon

Chopped fresh marjoram to taste

1 cup crème fraîche, sour cream or heavy cream

Freshly ground black pepper

2 slices dark rye bread, cut into small cubes

1 garlic clove

4 servings
815 calories per serving
Preparation time: about 2 hours

Rinse bones. Place in large saucepan with cold water and bring to simmer over low heat, uncovered or at most partially covered.

• Add meat, season broth with salt and return to simmer as slowly as possible. Cook slowly for 1 hour, partially covered; do not let broth boil or meat will dry out.

• Meanwhile, prepare vegetables. Peel potatoes, rinse and cut into small cubes. Peel and slice carrots; peel and dice celery root. Trim leek, leaving about ¼ of green part. Wash leek carefully and cut into rings. Peel, rinse and dice parsley root.

• Add vegetables to broth with celery leaves and parsley and cook 30 minutes longer.

• While vegetables cook, finely dice bacon. Place heavy ungreased skillet over low heat, add bacon cubes and cook, stirring frequently, until fat is rendered.

• Remove bones and meat from broth; discard bones. Either cut meat into small cubes and return to soup, or reserve for another use (it may be added to a salad, for instance).

• Coarsely mash vegetables with potato masher.

• Remove bacon from skillet with slotted spoon. Stir into soup with marjoram and crème fraîche; season with salt and pepper.

• Add bread cubes to skillet with bacon fat and sauté until golden brown, stirring frequently.

• Peel garlic and mash with a little salt. Add to bread cubes and cook briefly.

• Scatter bread cubes over soup with garlic and bacon fat and serve.

Tomato Cream Soup

This tastes best if made with fresh herbs. Use only the freshest milk and cream to ensure that they don't curdle when mixed with the tomatoes.

The tomato-puree base for this creamy soup can be prepared ahead and refrigerated or frozen; this is particularly appropriate during the summer, when sun-ripened tomatoes are plentiful and inexpensive. To finish the soup, simply reheat the puree and blend in the milk and cream.

1½ pounds ripe tomatoes
1 bunch soup greens
1 parsley root
1 onion
1 garlic clove
2 tablespoons (¼ stick) butter
1 bunch parsley, chopped
1 sprig rosemary
1 sprig thyme
1 lovage or celery leaf
Salt and pepper
1 teaspoon chicken broth granules
½ teaspoon sugar
3 cups milk
1 cup heavy cream

4 servings
390 calories per serving
Preparation time: about 1 hour

Blanch tomatoes in boiling water for 30 seconds. Plunge into cold water to stop cooking process; drain. Remove stem ends, halve and squeeze out seeds. Chop tomatoes.
• Finely chop soup greens. Peel and chop parsley root, onion and garlic.
• Melt butter in large saucepan over medium heat. Add onion and garlic and cook until translucent, stirring frequently. Add tomatoes, soup greens and parsley root and cook briefly.
• Add parsley, herb sprigs and lovage, cover and cook over low heat for 40 minutes.

• Remove herb sprigs. Transfer tomato mixture to blender and puree.
• Return puree to saucepan and bring to simmer, adding salt, broth granules, sugar and pepper.
• Transfer about ½ cup hot tomato puree to medium bowl and whisk in about 1 cup milk. Stir mixture back into saucepan. Blend in remaining milk and cream and heat gently.

Pichelstein One-Pot

A hearty one-pot meal that is easy to prepare.

3 ounces beef marrow
7 ounces each beef and pork shoulder or butt
7 ounces veal shoulder
7 ounces lamb shoulder
3 onions
10 to 11 ounces celery root
10 to 11 ounces carrots
1 scant pound boiling potatoes
½ head cabbage
Salt and freshly ground black pepper
½ bunch marjoram
2 to 3 cups water
1 bunch parsley

6 servings
535 calories per serving
Preparation time: about 2 hours

Rinse beef marrow under cold running water and blot dry with paper towels. Remove any veins or membranes with the tip of a sharp knife.

• Cut marrow into thin, even slices and arrange in a single layer on the bottom of a large flameproof casserole. (The marrow gives a wonderful aroma and flavor to the dish; as its fat renders out during cooking it also keeps the vegetables from burning.)
• Trim any fat and tendon from meat; slice meat thinly across the grain. Cut any very wide slices in half to make bite-size pieces.
• Trim roots from the peeled onions without separating the onion layers. Slice thinly, keeping slices as intact as possible.
• Peel celery root, cut into thin slices and halve or quarter slices as necessary. Peel or scrub carrots and slice thinly. Peel potatoes, wash well and blot thoroughly dry. Cut into thin, even slices.

• Trim and reserve outer cabbage leaves. Halve or quarter cabbage and cut out core with a sharp knife.

• Using a wedge-shaped cut, remove thick lower vein from each outer leaf of cabbage. Cut or tear leaves into wide strips.

• Layer meat and vegetables over marrow in casserole. Season each layer with salt, pepper and a few marjoram leaves.
• Add water to come ½ to ¾ of the way up through contents of casserole. Cover and bring to simmer. Adjust heat as necessary so that mixture simmers gently for about 1½ hours; toward end of cooking uncover, raise heat and boil off excess liquid, if desired.
• Meanwhile, rinse parsley, shake dry and chop finely. Add half of parsley to stew at end of cooking time; sprinkle remaining parsley over top. Serve piping hot. This dish is particularly good with dark rye bread and salt sticks.

Variation: Irish Stew

This is made with somewhat different ingredients, but the cooking method is the same. For 6 servings, slice 1¾ pounds boneless lean lamb. Peel and slice 1 to 1¼ pounds boiling potatoes and 1 generous pound onions. Beginning with potatoes, layer ingredients in large flameproof casserole, seasoning as desired with salt, pepper and chopped thyme or a sprinkling of caraway seed. Add 1 to 2 small bay leaves and finish with a layer of potato slices.
Pour in 2 to 3 cups hot meat broth, cover and bring to simmer. Adjust heat so that stew cooks gently for about 1½ hours. Chop 1 bunch parsley and add about ¾ of it to stew; sprinkle with remaining parsley just before serving.

Variation: New-Style Irish Stew

This is much like traditional Irish stew, but it has a few additions that slightly modify the quantities of the ingredients. Slice 1¾ pounds boneless lean lamb. Slice or chop ½ head cabbage, 1 generous pound boiling potatoes, 3 to 4 carrots and 4 to 5 onions. Layer meat and vegetables in casserole and season with salt, pepper, caraway seed and bay leaf. Add 2 to 3 cups broth as above, cover and cook gently for 1½ hours. Mix in chopped parsley; sprinkle additional parsley over top before serving.
Tip: These three stews will be more flavorful if the meats are sautéed separately in hot lard or in a mixture of butter and oil before they are layered with the vegetables. You may also wish to add a bit of smoked ham, thinly sliced garlic sausage or a few mushrooms—the general rule being, if it tastes good, why not?

Culinary historians have long argued over the exact origin of this traditional German dish. But there's no dispute over the ingredients, and this hearty, honest *Eintopf*, is suitable for both family and company dinners.

Minestrone

This is essentially a vegetable stew.

5 ounces dried white beans
3 ounces bacon
1 onion
2 garlic cloves
8 ounces carrots
2 parsley roots
2 celery stalks
1 leek
8 ounces regular, Savoy or Chinese cabbage
1 generous pound fresh green peas (in the pod)
2¼ pounds fresh lima or fava beans (in the pod)
¼ cup cold-pressed olive oil
1 pound, 10 ounces ripe tomatoes
2 quarts meat broth
1 bay leaf
1 sprig rosemary
1 bunch parsley
½ cup long-grain rice
Salt and freshly ground black pepper

6 servings
400 calories per serving
Preparation time: about 1¾ hours
Soaking time: about 8 hours

Rinse and sort dried beans. Place in saucepan, cover generously with cold water and soak for about 8 hours.
• Place beans and soaking water over high heat and bring to boil. Reduce heat, cover and simmer 50 minutes.
• Meanwhile, chop bacon, trimming away any rind. Finely chop onion; chop garlic.
• Peel and slice carrots; peel and chop parsley roots. Remove any tough strings from celery with vegetable peeler and cut celery into ¼-inch pieces. Clean leek thoroughly; trim, leaving tender green parts. Cut into even rings.

• Remove tough outer leaves from cabbage. Quarter the head and remove core with a diagonal cut. Separate and wash leaves; cut away thick inner ribs. Chop leaves coarsely.
• Shell peas and lima beans. Place in sieve and rinse well; shake dry.

• Heat olive oil in large saucepan over medium-low heat. Add bacon and stir frequently until meat is crisp and fat foams slightly.
• Meanwhile, blanch tomatoes in boiling water for 30 seconds. Plunge into cold water to stop cooking process; drain. Remove stem ends, halve and squeeze out seeds. Chop tomatoes finely or purée in blender or processor.
• Add onion to saucepan and cook until translucent and golden. Add garlic and cook just until barely colored. (Garlic should always be cooked briefly and over moderate heat, as it browns quickly and this makes it bitter.)
• Drain cooked white beans in sieve.

• Add peas, lima beans, carrot, parsley root, celery, leek and cabbage to saucepan and cook 5 minutes over medium heat, stirring frequently to prevent scorching. As soon as

vegetables have brightened slightly in color and are coated with a thin layer of oil, add drained white beans.

• Add broth and bring to boil over high heat. Stir in tomato.
• Tie bay leaf, rosemary and parsley together with string and add to soup. Cover and cook gently over low heat for 20 minutes.
• Meanwhile, place rice in sieve and rinse until water runs clear (if you would like a thicker soup, leave rice unrinsed; the starch clinging to the grains will give the minestrone more body).
• Stir rice into soup, return to simmer and cook 20 to 25 minutes longer over gentle heat.
• Remove herb bundle. Season soup with salt and pepper, transfer to heated tureen and serve hot, garnished with freshly grated Parmesan cheese or chopped mixed fresh herbs. Accompany with French or Italian bread.

Real Italian *minestrone* is a vegetable soup with such satisfying additions as rice, noodles or barley. (Other less substantial soups are variously known as *minestre* or *zuppe*.) Prepare your minestrone as Italian cooks do, using a large assortment of vegetables depending on what the market has to offer. For a winter version, add more legumes and use frozen vegetables.

Salade Niçoise

A classic with countless variations.

1 pound boiling potatoes
Salt
1 pound slender green beans or *haricots verts*
1 small onion
8 mixed black and green olives, pitted
1 can (2 ounces) anchovy fillets
Pinch of sugar
3 tablespoons white or red wine vinegar
Freshly ground black pepper
6 to 7 tablespoons cold-pressed olive oil
4 ripe tomatoes
2 tablespoons small capers

4 servings
340 calories per serving
Preparation time: about 1 hour
Marinating time: about 30 minutes

Scrub potatoes and cook in their jackets in salted water just until tender; do not overcook. Plunge into cold water, drain and cool.

- Trim ends of beans; remove strings if necessary.
- Bring large saucepan of generously salted water to vigorous boil for 3 minutes, then add beans; water should not stop boiling.
- Add 2 or 3 handfuls of ice cubes to a large bowl of cold water.

- After 8 to 10 minutes remove beans from boiling water with slotted spoon and immediately plunge into ice water, which will stop cooking process and preserve bright green color of beans. When cooled through, drain beans and blot dry.
- Halve onion and cut into paper-thin slices.
- Drain olives and anchovies; if using salt-packed anchovies, rinse briefly under cold water, then drain. Bone fillets if necessary.

- Combine about ½ teaspoon salt and sugar in mixing bowl. Add vinegar and whisk until both salt and sugar are completely dissolved; this is important, as undissolved particles will become coated with oil and thereby lose their flavoring power.

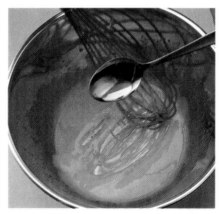

- Add pepper to vinegar mixture. Add oil in slow stream, whisking constantly; it must form a homogeneous emulsion with the vinegar.
- Slice potatoes and combine with beans and onion in serving bowl. Add dressing and toss lightly to coat. Cover and let stand about 30 minutes.
- Blanch tomatoes in boiling water for 30 seconds. Plunge into cold water to stop cooking process; drain. Remove stem ends, halve and squeeze out seeds. Cut tomatoes into narrow strips. Combine with olives and anchovies, add to salad and toss gently.
- Drain capers and sprinkle over salad. Serve with French bread.

Tip: You may wish to season the dressing with chopped fresh herbs. Parsley is very good, along with a few basil leaves or some oregano. A hint of thyme also lends an interesting note.

Variation:
Greek Farmer's Salad

This, too, is among the most popular summer salads, served in seemingly every restaurant and ubiquitous at picnics and barbecues. As with *salade Niçoise*, there is little agreement as to which of the innumerable variations is the best and most authentic, so try this recipe: For 4 servings, remove stem, seeds and membranes from 1 green bell pepper. Rinse pepper, dry and cut into narrow strips. Cut 1 large mild onion into thin rings or strips. Cut out stem ends from 3 tomatoes and cut tomatoes into wedges. Rinse and dry 1 small cucumber; halve lengthwise and scoop out seeds with melon baller or teaspoon; slice cucumber. Drain 3 to 4 ounces black olives. Combine ½ teaspoon salt and a small pinch of sugar in mixing bowl. Add 2 to 3 tablespoons red or white wine vinegar and whisk until salt and sugar are completely dissolved. Add a generous amount of freshly ground black pepper and 5 to 6 tablespoons cold-pressed olive oil and whisk until well blended. Combine vegetables and olives in serving bowl and sprinkle with about 7 ounces crumbled feta cheese. Pour dressing over salad and toss lightly but thoroughly to blend. Sprinkle with a scant teaspoon of crushed dried oregano and serve.

Tip: We recommend adding a bit of pressed garlic to the dressing, or slicing a garlic clove very thinly and adding the slices to the finished salad. Basil, thyme, dill or a tiny bit of fresh mint is also delicious here.

Salade Niçoise is ever-present on restaurant menus but you never know quite what to expect. The classic formula calls for only green beans, potatoes, tomatoes, olives, anchovy fillets and capers, but many people maintain that the salad is much better with the addition of tuna fish and hard-cooked eggs. Others wouldn't dream of omitting celery, bell pepper and cucumber slices, or always garnish the finished dish with tender leaf lettuce.

Italian-Style Vegetables

A two-part first course or light summer meal with Mediterranean flavors.

1 each green, yellow and red bell peppers
2 small zucchini
1 medium eggplant
Salt
1½ cups (about) cold-pressed olive oil
4 garlic cloves
2 sprigs rosemary
½ bunch thyme
¼ cup white wine vinegar
Freshly ground black pepper
2 bunches leeks or scallions
1 pound fresh mushrooms
1 bunch tarragon
½ bunch parsley
1 lemon
1 cup chicken broth
½ cup dry white wine
1 bay leaf
8 white peppercorns

8 servings
350 calories per serving
Preparation time: about 1½ hours
Marinating time: at least 6 hours

Preheat oven to 475°F. Wash and dry all vegetables and herbs.

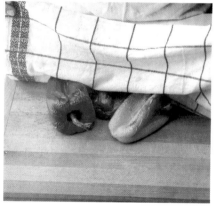

• Roast peppers until skin blisters and wrinkles, about 20 minutes. Remove from oven and cover with damp kitchen towel.

• Trim ends of zucchini (do not peel). Using a sharp knife, cut zucchini into ¼-inch-thick crosswise or diagonal slices.

• Trim ends of eggplant. Halve lengthwise, then cut crosswise into ¼-inch-thick slices. Place in bowl or colander, sprinkle with salt and toss. Let stand 10 minutes to allow salt to draw out moisture.
• Peel peppers with the help of a paring knife (skin will peel easily where it is blistered; where there are no blisters a bit of flesh may come away with the skin). Trim away stem ends. Quarter peppers lengthwise and remove seeds and membranes.
• Pat eggplant slices dry with paper towels to remove excess moisture and salt.
• Heat a heavy dry skillet until a drop of water sprinkled onto the bottom sizzles and evaporates. Add a bit of olive oil and heat until oil loses its surface tension and flows freely.
• Add eggplant slices in batches and sauté until golden on both sides, adding more oil as necessary and heating each new addition of oil before adding vegetables. Remove slices and drain on several layers of paper towel.
• Slice garlic. Strip leaves from rosemary and thyme stems.
• One at a time, sauté zucchini and peppers in batches in olive oil and drain on paper towels. Combine with eggplant in large bowl.
• Add half of garlic to skillet and sauté until translucent but not colored. Add rosemary and thyme leaves and sauté very briefly. Add vinegar and season with black pepper to taste.
• Add about 6 tablespoons olive oil and heat almost to boiling; do not bring to full boil or allow oil to smoke. Pour contents of skillet over vegetables.

• For second vegetable mixture, trim root ends of leeks or scallions and cut away tough green parts.

• Trim stem ends of mushrooms and wipe mushrooms clean; rinse briefly only if absolutely necessary. Halve or quarter large mushrooms.
• Chop tarragon and parsley leaves; set aside. Reserve stems.
• Wash lemon in hot water and dry. Remove a small, paper-thin slice of rind (colored part only) with a sharp knife. Halve and juice lemon; set rind and juice aside.
• Heat about ¼ cup olive oil over medium-low heat in large skillet or saucepan. Add leeks or scallions and cook, shaking pan frequently, until translucent but not browned. Remove from pan with slotted spoon.
• Add mushrooms to skillet and increase heat to medium-high. Sauté, shaking pan frequently, until mushrooms are somewhat darkened but not browned. Return leeks to skillet and stir in remaining garlic.
• Pour in chicken broth and wine and bring to simmer. Add tarragon and parsley stems, lemon rind and juice, bay leaf and peppercorns and cook 10 minutes.
• Discard herb stems and lemon rind. Using slotted spoon, transfer vegetables to another bowl.
• Place broth mixture over high heat and boil uncovered until reduced to about 1 cup.
• Add parsley and tarragon leaves, cook for a moment and pour mixture over mushrooms and leeks. Let stand at least 6 hours before serving.

Antipasti, the colorful mixed appetizers so well known in Italian cooking, are unthinkable without marinated vegetables. Spain, Greece and southern France offer an array of similar preparations. Of course, they need not be limited to first courses; they are also excellent side dishes with sautéed or grilled meats, and cold roasts. We offer here two easy mixtures that can also be used as base recipes if you wish to substitute other vegetables.

Quiche Lorraine

A hearty ham-flavored tart, particularly good with a fruity young white wine.

1¾ cups all-purpose flour

5 eggs

Salt

1 to 2 tablespoons ice water

10 tablespoons (1¼ sticks) chilled butter

8 to 9 ounces bacon, thinly sliced

3 to 4 ounces Emmental or Gruyère cheese, thinly sliced

1 cup heavy cream

Sweet paprika

Freshly ground white pepper

Butter to dot top of quiche

8 servings
690 calories per serving
Preparation time: about 50 minutes
Cooling time: 30 minutes

Mound flour on work surface. Make a well in center and add 1 egg, pinch of salt and 1 tablespoon ice water. Cut 8 tablespoons butter into small bits and sprinkle around edge of well.

- Combine these ingredients quickly with cool fingertips to form smooth dough, adding only as much ice water as is needed to hold dough together. Form into ball and flatten into thick disc. Wrap in foil or plastic and chill 30 minutes to help make baked crust crisp.
- Meanwhile, halve bacon slices crosswise. Melt remaining 2 tablespoons butter in large skillet over medium heat; do not brown.
- Add bacon to skillet and stir frequently until fat is translucent. Remove and drain on paper towels.
- Adjust oven rack to second position from bottom and preheat oven to 400°F. Have ready a 10-inch springform pan.
- Cut cheese slices into quarters.
- Roll out chilled dough on sheet of aluminum foil to about ⅛-inch thickness.

Cut out dough circle using springform bottom as guide. Cut a 1½-inch-wide strip of dough for side of tart and a ½-inch-wide strip of the same thickness to cover seam between side and bottom crusts.

- Lift dough off foil and line bottom and side of springform. Press narrow dough strip into crack where the two pieces meet. Prick bottom of crust with a fork.
- Alternate slices of bacon and cheese in overlapping pattern on bottom of crust.

- Place remaining 4 eggs in mixing bowl and whisk to blend.

- Blend in cream. Season with paprika, pepper and a generous pinch of salt. Pour egg mixture into crust and shake pan lightly to distribute evenly.

- Dot top of quiche with butter.
- Bake about 30 minutes, or until edges are browned, filling is almost firm and a wooden pick inserted in center comes out clean. If top of quiche browns too quickly, reduce oven temperature a bit and cover the tart with foil.
- Let cool slightly, then cut quiche into 8 wedges and serve warm with a tossed salad.

**Variation:
German Onion Tart**

Prepare dough as for Quiche Lorraine, replacing butter with chilled lard and adding a generous pinch of cayenne pepper. While dough is chilling, slice 2¼ pounds onions into rings. Sauté in batches in about 7 tablespoons butter over medium heat, stirring frequently, until translucent and half-tender. Chop 9 ounces Black Forest ham and cook over medium heat in another skillet until fat is rendered. Combine ham pieces and onion and cool to lukewarm. Whisk 3 egg yolks with 1 cup sour cream, 1 scant teaspoon sweet or medium-hot paprika, and freshly ground white pepper, ground caraway seed and salt to taste. Combine with onion mixture. Line 10-inch springform with dough as for Quiche Lorraine. Add filling and bake in preheated 400°F oven for about 30 minutes. Serve warm.

In France, a quiche is always thin-crusted and filled with a rich custard. Surely the finest version of this classic dish is Quiche Lorraine, traditionally made with a tender, buttery crust and a piquant filling of bacon and cheese covered with eggs and cream. You can vary the quiche by adding onions or fresh herbs, or by substituting milk for half the cream. Quiche Lorraine is delicious with wine or cocktails, and can be prepared ahead and even frozen.

Spinach Gratin

This first course tastes best when made with tender young spinach leaves. Even if the selection of fresh spinach isn't ideal, don't substitute frozen.

An easy, sophisticated Italian antipasto.

8 to 9 ounces fresh spinach

Salt

1 onion

1 garlic clove

3 to 4 ounces boiled ham, thinly sliced

4 ounces mozzarella cheese

1 tablespoon cold-pressed olive oil

½ lemon

Freshly ground white pepper

Butter for baking shells or dish

4 servings
230 calories per serving
Preparation time: about 40 minutes

Carefully sort spinach and wash in several changes of water. Shake thoroughly dry and remove large, tough stems.
• Adjust oven rack to second position from top and preheat oven to 475°F.
• Blanch spinach in batches in large pot of rapidly boiling salted water for about 45 seconds, holding leaves under water with skimmer or slotted spoon. Lift leaves out with the skimmer and drop briefly into large bowl of ice water to cool (this will preserve spinach's bright green color). Drain well and chop.

• Finely chop onion and garlic. Cut ham into fine strips and mozzarella into small cubes.
• Heat olive oil in skillet over medium heat. Add onion and garlic and cook until translucent. Add ham and cook, stirring, until slightly crisp.
• Squeeze juice from lemon half and sprinkle over ham mixture. Add spinach and heat through, stirring. Season with salt and pepper.
• Butter 4 scallop shells or a baking dish. Add spinach mixture and top with mozzarella cubes. Bake until cheese is melted and golden brown, about 15 minutes. Serve immediately.

Variation:
Spinach with Pine Nuts

Prepare 1 pound fresh spinach as above—stem, blanch, plunge into ice water, drain and chop. Finely chop 1 onion and 1 garlic clove. Heat 2 tablespoons olive oil in skillet, add onion and garlic and cook over medium heat until translucent. Add spinach, season with salt and freshly ground white pepper and heat through, stirring. Toast 1 ounce (about 3 tablespoons) pine nuts in ungreased heavy small skillet until golden brown, shaking skillet frequently. Transfer spinach to heated serving bowl and sprinkle with pine nuts.

Eggplant with Yogurt Cream

Borage is an annual herb with cucumber-scented leaves and star-shaped blue flowers. It is easily grown from seed; try a nursery for seeds or plants.

A piquant first course or light summer meal.

1 pound, 10 ounces slender eggplants
Salt
½ cucumber
1 tomato
1 bunch chives
10 (about) borage leaves
1 cup yogurt
1 cup crème fraîche or sour cream
3 garlic cloves
1 teaspoon cold-pressed olive oil
Freshly ground black pepper
All-purpose flour for coating eggplant
Olive oil for frying

4 servings
400 calories per serving
Preparation time: about 1 hour

Wash and dry eggplants; trim ends. cut diagonally into slices the thickness of a finger. Sprinkle with salt on both sides and let stand about 10 minutes to draw out juices.

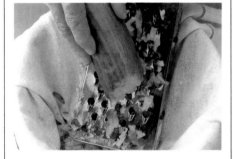

- Wash and dry cucumber. Line bowl with kitchen towel and shred in cucumber, using coarse holes of grater. Salt lightly and let stand to drain.
- Blanch tomato in boiling water for 30 seconds. Plunge into cold water to stop cooking process; drain. Peel, stem, seed and finely dice tomato. Rinse chives and borage; shake dry and mince.
- Blend yogurt and crème fraîche. Force garlic through press into yogurt mixture. Add diced tomato, herbs and olive oil and season with salt and pepper.
- Squeeze excess moisture from cucumber with towel. Blend cucumber into sauce with tomato. Cover and chill until ready to serve.
- Pat eggplant slices dry and dust both sides with flour.
- Heat a few tablespoons olive oil in large skillet. Add eggplant slices in batches and fry on both sides until golden brown, adding more oil to skillet as necessary. Drain eggplant on paper towels. Divide eggplant among serving plates, spoon sauce over and serve at once.

Fish Provençal

This preparation results in tender fish with marvelous aroma and flavor.

1 small eggplant (8 to 9 ounces)
Salt
1 onion
4 garlic cloves
8 to 9 ounces zucchini
1 green bell pepper
1 red bell pepper
1 pound tomatoes
½ generous cup cold-pressed olive oil
1 bunch parsley
4 sprigs thyme
1 sprig rosemary
1 to 2 sprigs sage
1 whole dressed sea bass (about 3¼ pounds)
Freshly ground white pepper
Juice of ½ lemon
2 bay leaves
½ cup dry white wine
Additional olive oil
1 bunch basil

4 servings
770 calories per serving
Preparation time: about 1½ hours

Wash, dry and trim ends of eggplant; cut into ¾-inch slices. Arrange in single layer on platter and sprinkle with salt on both sides. Let stand until surface of slices is covered with droplets of moisture, then pat dry with paper towels.
• Halve onion lengthwise and cut into small, even dice.

• Cut garlic into very thin lengthwise slices. Finely chop half of slices; cut remainder into thin, even julienne.
• Wash and dry zucchini; trim ends. Cut zucchini into even slices.
• Stem bell peppers and quarter lengthwise; remove membranes and seeds. Rinse peppers, blot dry and cut into strips.

• Pour boiling water over tomatoes to blanche. Peel, stem, seed and cut into strips or cubes.
• Heat about ⅔ of oil in large deep skillet or saucepan. Add eggplant slices in batches and fry on both sides until golden brown. Drain on several layers of paper towel.
• Heat remaining olive oil in same pan; add onion and cook, stirring, until translucent. Add chopped garlic and cook about 30 seconds longer.

• Add pepper strips and cook 5 minutes, then add zucchini and cook, stirring, 1 to 2 minutes. Add tomatoes and cook another 1 to 2 minutes; remove from heat.
• Adjust oven rack to lowest position and preheat oven to 425°F. Rinse herbs and shake dry. Finely chop parsley. Strip leaves from 2 thyme sprigs and mix with a few rosemary leaves; set aside. Cut sage leaves into strips. Add chopped herbs to vegetable mixture.

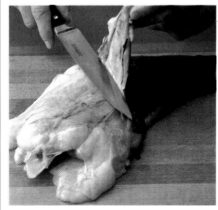

• Rinse fish and pat dry. Slit skin along spine with sharp knife and remove skin by pulling off from front to back.

• Loosen fillets from sides of fish using sharp knife held parallel to bones and as close to bones as possible.
• Insert garlic julienne at intervals into fillets. Season with salt and pepper; sprinkle with lemon juice.
• Arrange eggplant slices in bottom of baking dish. Place fish atop eggplant. Sprinkle with reserved thyme and rosemary; add bay leaves. Spread vegetable mixture over top and season with salt and pepper.

• Pour wine into one side of dish and sprinkle vegetables with olive oil. Cover and bake 40 minutes.
• Meanwhile, rinse basil and shake dry. Discard stems. Garnish top of casserole with basil leaves or sprigs and serve immediately with French bread.

Fish remains tender and juicy when baked in the oven protected by layers of flavorful summer vegetables and herbs. Prepare this in an attractive casserole that can be brought steaming hot to the table. If you can't find sea bass, substitute another firm-fleshed fish such as rock cod, rockfish, snapper, lake trout, perch or whiting.

Homestyle Herring Fillets

Though served cold, this is richly flavorful and satisfying.

Herring, formerly thought of as poor people's food, is now considered a delicacy. The most delicious of all is *matjes* herring, caught while still immature and available fresh only in early summer. For this recipe you can use either *matjes* fillets or stronger-flavored salt herring.

| 12 herring fillets, salted or *matjes* |
| 3 onions |
| 1 cup water |
| 1 cup white wine vinegar |
| 8 black peppercorns |
| 1 tablespoon mustard seed |
| 8 allspice berries |
| 3 whole cloves |
| 2 bay leaves |
| 4 parsley stems |
| 2 tart apples (10 to 11 ounces) |
| 1 bunch chives |
| ½ cup heavy cream |
| 1 cup sour cream |
| Pinch of sugar |
| Salt and freshly ground white pepper |

6 servings
560 calories per serving
Preparation time: about 45 minutes
Marinating time: 8 hours altogether
Soaking time (if necessary): 6 to 8 hours

Place herring fillets in large bowl and add enough cold water to cover by several inches. Soak herring, changing

water occasionally, until water is no longer very salty when tasted. (Note: soaking is not necessary if you are using mild *matjes* herring.)

• For marinade, cut 1 onion into thin rings. Combine water, vinegar, 6 peppercorns, mustard seed, allspice berries, 2 cloves, 1 bay leaf and washed, dried parsley stems in nonaluminum saucepan and bring to boil. Add onion rings, reduce heat to low and simmer 1 minute. Remove from heat and cool completely.

• Cut herring fillets into pieces 1 to 1½ inches wide. Place in glass or ceramic bowl, pour marinade over, cover and chill 6 hours.

• Cut remaining 2 onions into thin rings. Peel and core apples and cut into small pieces. Spoon some of marinade over apples to keep them from discoloring.

• Rinse and dry chives; snip into tiny rings (the finer the chives are cut the better they will release their flavor).

• For sauce, combine heavy cream and sour cream and mix with remaining peppercorns, cloves, sugar and salt and pepper to taste. Stir in chives, reserving a little for garnish.

• Drain fish and apple pieces.

• Layer herring, onion rings and apple pieces in shallow dish, spooning sauce between layers. Lay bay leaf on top and pour remaining sauce over all.

• Cover and let stand in a cool place (preferably not in the refrigerator) for about 2 hours. Garnish with reserved chives. Serve with boiled or fried potatoes or with dark rye bread and butter.

Foil-Baked Fish

This terrific dish takes less than an hour to prepare. You can, of course, use other fish instead of cod: Trout, striped or sea bass, haddock, snapper and rockfish are all possibilities.

Ideal for a company dinner.

1 whole dressed cod (about 3¼ pounds)
Salt and freshly ground white pepper
Juice of ½ lemon
1 shallot
1 garlic clove
2 carrots
2 leeks
1 fennel bulb
2 tablespoons (¼ stick) butter
2 sprigs dill
½ bunch parsley
3 tablespoons medium-dry Sherry
1⅓ cups crème fraîche or sour cream
1 bunch chives, finely chopped

6 servings
700 calories per serving
Preparation time: about 50 minutes

Cut away fins from fish. Rinse and dry fish; sprinkle with salt, pepper and lemon juice.

• Finely chop shallot and garlic. Peel carrots and slice thinly. Trim and clean leeks and cut into thin rings. Trim fennel tops; cut bulb into strips.

• Melt butter in skillet. Add shallot, garlic, carrots, leek and fennel bulb and cook until partially tender. Transfer vegetables to large sheet of foil. Stuff fish with dill, a few parsley sprigs and fennel tops and set on top of vegetables.

• Position rack in center of oven and preheat oven to 425°F.

• Chop remaining parsley. Mix with Sherry and half of crème fraîche and pour over fish.

• Fold foil over fish and roll together at edges. Fold edges up 2 or 3 times to seal.

• Place foil packet on roasting rack and bake 30 minutes. Open and pour sauce into pan; keep fish warm.

• Blend remaining crème fraîche into sauce and cook uncovered until thickened. Stir in chives.

Crusty Roast Pork

Foolproof, even for beginning cooks.

1 fresh pork shoulder or butt (about 2¼ pounds), with rind
3 cups (about) boiling water
10 to 11 ounces meat bones, sawed into small pieces (have your butcher do this)
2 onions
1 carrot
1 small piece (about 3 ounces) celery root
3 tomatoes
2 garlic cloves
1 teaspoon caraway seed
1 bay leaf
Salt
1 teaspoon coarsely crushed black pepper
1 teaspoon tomato paste
1 teaspoon cornstarch

4 servings
780 calories per serving
Preparation time: about 3 hours

When you purchase the meat, be sure the layer of fat under the rind is an even ¼ inch or so thick and that it completely covers one surface of the meat. (This will ensure that the meat came from a well-fed animal, that it will have good flavor and that it will not shrink excessively during cooking.)
• Adjust oven rack to lowest position and preheat oven to 475°F.

• Score pork rind and fat in parallel lines to form diamonds; be sure not to cut into meat.
• Place meat in roasting pan fat side down and add about ½ cup boiling water. Place in oven until water is evaporated and some of fat is rendered, about 15 minutes.

• Meanwhile, rinse and dry bones. Peel and coarsely chop onions, carrot and celery root. Stem and coarsely chop tomatoes. Halve garlic cloves.
• Turn pork fat side up. Add bones to roasting pan and roast until lightly browned, about 10 to 15 minutes.
• Add prepared vegetables, caraway, bay leaf and salt and pepper to pan and roast until vegetables start to color, about 10 minutes, stirring frequently with wooden spatula to cook vegetables evenly. Remove pan from oven; reduce oven temperature to 425°F.
• Stir in tomato paste and about ⅓ cup boiling water, scraping bottom of pan with spatula to loosen browned bits.
• Place pan over direct heat and boil until liquid is nearly evaporated. Add another ⅓ cup boiling water and again boil until liquid has almost disappeared.
• Add remaining boiling water and return roast to oven until cooked to an internal temperature of 160°F to 170°F, basting occasionally with pan juices and adding more water (or broth) to pan if mixture seems dry.
• Wrap meat in foil and keep warm in turned-off oven.

• Strain contents of roasting pan into saucepan, pressing lightly on vegetables to extract all liquid. Reserve vegetables to serve with meat if you wish. Place saucepan over high heat and boil, uncovered, to concentrate flavor.

• Mix cornstarch with enough cold water to form a fluid paste and whisk into gravy. Boil until thickened, whisking constantly. Season with salt and pepper.
• Slice meat diagonally across grain.
• Arrange meat slices on heated platter. Pour some of gravy around (not over) meat and arrange desired side-dish vegetables (or vegetables that cooked with meat) around edges of platter. Pass remaining gravy separately. Especially good accompaniments are boiled potatoes or potato dumplings, red or green cabbage, cauliflower, Brussels sprouts or broccoli.

Variation:
Baked Ham

This is best made with a small whole cooked ham (about 5½ pounds); it will serve 8 to 10. Score ham rind and fat into diamonds and stud with whole cloves. Pour water (or a mixture of water and white wine) around ham and bake in preheated 400°F to 425°F oven about 1 hour. Halfway through baking, spread meat with a glaze made of honey, orange juice, paprika, ginger, curry powder and Cognac *or* with a mixture of apple jelly, Port, mustard, cinnamon and allspice.

Roast pork is as beloved for its sensational aroma as for its crisp, succulent skin, not to mention the delicious gravy that can be made from the drippings. Some cooks flavor the meat with wine; others enrich the gravy with cream. In this typically Bavarian treatment the gravy is made particularly flavorful with the addition of extra meat bones. Cuts of fresh ham butt (from the upper or lower side of the porker's hind leg) make very lean and tender roasts; though fattier, shoulder cuts are also excellent. These parts are not always sold with the rind, so it is advisable to order the meat ahead of time.

Pork Tenderloin in Puff Pastry

This fabulous dish is well worth the time it takes to prepare.

1 package (17¼ ounces) frozen puff pastry

2 center-cut pork tenderloins, about 12 ounces each

1½ tablespoons vegetable oil

1½ tablespoons butter

Salt and freshly ground black pepper

1 shallot

1 garlic clove

14 ounces fresh mushrooms

3 ounces mixed fresh parsley, tarragon and chervil

2 sprigs thyme

½ cup heavy cream or crème fraîche

Salt and freshly ground white pepper

All-purpose flour for rolling pastry

1 egg

3 to 4 ounces boiled ham, thinly sliced

2 egg yolks, lightly beaten

4 servings
1000 calories per serving
Preparation time: about 1¼ hours
Thawing time: about 2 hours
Refrigeration time: 30 minutes

Remove pastry from package, separate sheets and thaw at room temperature. Unfold when fully thawed.

• Trim any fat or membrane from tenderloins; pat meat thoroughly dry with paper towels.

• Heat oil and butter in large skillet over high heat. Add meat and brown well on all sides. Remove meat from skillet, season with salt and black pepper and let cool; reserve fat in skillet.

• Mince shallot and garlic. Trim and clean mushrooms; mince. Rinse herbs and shake dry. Strip thyme leaves from stems. Finely chop all herbs.

• Sauté shallot and garlic in fat in skillet until translucent. Add mushrooms and cook over medium heat, stirring frequently, until all liquid is evaporated.

• Gradually add cream, continuing to cook over high heat until mixture is thick and spreadable. Season with salt and white pepper, stir in herbs and cool to lukewarm.

• Adjust oven rack to second position from bottom and preheat oven to 400°F.

• Lightly flour work surface and rolling pin.

• Sprinkle one pastry sheet lightly with water. Lay second sheet on top and roll out with light, even strokes in all directions. (The layers of butter and dough must not be mashed together or dough will not rise properly.) Trim a piece of dough to cut decorative shapes for garnish; refrigerate this smaller piece.

• Blend whole egg into mushroom mixture. Spread mushrooms in center of pastry and arrange ham slices on top of mushrooms, overlapping edges. Place tenderloins on ham.

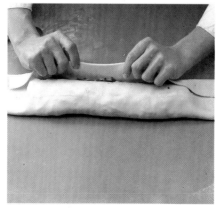

• Bring up one long edge of pastry to cover meat and mushroom filling. Brush with beaten egg yolks. Fold in short ends

of pastry and brush with yolk. Bring second long side over to form a package and press lightly to seal.

• Carefully turn "package" seam side down. Transfer to baking sheet and refrigerate 30 minutes (chilling helps make baked pastry crisp and flaky).

• Cut decorative leaf or other shapes from reserved dough strip. Press onto dough packet using egg yolk as "glue." Brush with additional egg yolk.

• Rinse baking sheet in cold water. Slide pastry-wrapped meat onto sheet with wide spatula.

• Bake 30 minutes, then turn off oven, open oven door halfway and let rest in oven 10 minutes longer.

• Cut into ¾-inch slices; this is most easily done if you first cut through pastry layer with a sharp serrated knife, then slice meat with a carving knife. Serve with cooked fresh vegetables or a salad.

One of the best-known dishes of classic French cuisine—tender filet mignon, spread with an aromatic mushroom filling and wrapped in crisp puff pastry—is named in honor of the Duke of Wellington, who helped to defeat Napoleon at Waterloo. Here we present a thriftier but just as delicious variation. Purchase two pork tenderloins of the same thickness so that they cook evenly. The herbs *must* be fresh; if you cannot get fresh chervil and tarragon, substitute all parsley.

Stuffed Pork Chops

A sophisticated dish that is simple to prepare.

4 pork chops, ¾ to 1¼ inches thick
Freshly ground white pepper
3 ripe but firm pears
1 tablespoon fresh lemon juice
5 ounces Roquefort cheese
¼ cup Cognac or pear *eau de vie*
2 tablespoons green peppercorns
2 tablespoons vegetable oil
4 teaspoons butter
Salt and freshly ground black pepper
½ cup dry white wine
½ cup heavy cream
Cayenne pepper
Pinch of sugar

4 servings
900 calories per serving
Preparation time: about 30 minutes

Wipe meat with damp towel to remove any clinging bits of bone.

• Insert a very sharp knife halfway up boneless side of chops; with even pressure, cut pocket in meat almost to bone. Sprinkle insides of pockets lightly with pepper.
• Peel, core and finely chop pears. Immediately sprinkle with some of the lemon juice to prevent discoloration.

• Place 3 to 4 ounces Roquefort in bowl and mash with fork, gradually adding a few drops of Cognac or *eau de vie*; mixture should be smooth and malleable but not too soft. Blend in green peppercorns and pear.
• Stuff pockets in meat with some of filling, securing each with 2 toothpicks (picks should, if possible, pierce fat layer around edge of meat, not meat itself).

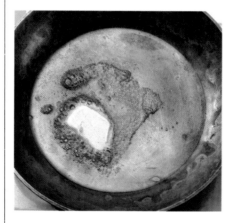

• Heat large skillet, then add oil. As soon as oil is hot, add butter and allow to melt. Arrange chops in pan without overlapping.
• Sauté chops over medium heat about 4 minutes per side, then remove from skillet, season with salt and pepper and keep warm on heated platter.

• Mix remaining lemon juice and wine into the fat and any melted cheese in skillet. Scrape up browned bits from bottom of skillet with spatula, then pour in cream and cook until reduced slightly, stirring.
• Add remaining cheese-pear mixture and cook, stirring, until sauce flows from spoon in a thick, creamy stream.
• Crumble remaining Roquefort and whisk into sauce. Season with salt, pepper, cayenne, sugar and remaining Cognac.

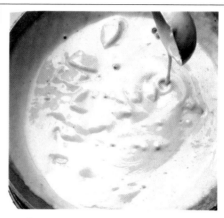

• Pour sauce around chops and serve at once. Good accompaniments are a green salad and French bread or parsley potatoes.

Variation: Stuffed Pork Chops *Cordon Bleu*

Cut pockets in pork chops as above. Place 1 slice each boiled ham and Emmental or Gruyère cheese in each pocket. Close pockets with toothpicks. Season meat with salt and pepper and coat with flour, pressing flour into meat. Beat 1 egg with 2 tablespoons milk, cream or water. Briefly dip floured chops into egg, then roll in fine dry breadcrumbs, pressing them in well. Sauté chops in butter or in a mixture of butter and oil.

Variation: Veal *Cordon Bleu*

For this beloved classic you may either cut pockets into veal chops as above or, even simpler, use 2 small, thin veal scallops per serving. Flatten scallops with the balls of your thumbs. Lay 1 slice each of ham and cheese on a scallop and cover with a second veal scallop. Secure with toothpicks, season with salt and pepper, coat with flour, egg and breadcrumbs and sauté in butter. Serve with lemon slices, if you wish.

Pork chops are among the most popular cuts of meat, and with good reason: They are flavorful and relatively lean, they require only brief cooking and—certainly important—they're quite inexpensive. Moreover, they lend themselves to many different preparations. They are delicious simply sautéed with salt, pepper and perhaps a bit of lemon juice, or they can be breaded, sauced in various ways, or stuffed. If they haven't been coated with a sauce, pork chops are also excellent cold, served with good bread and mustard or horseradish.

Half-and-Half Goulash

In our list of favorite dishes this is right near the top.

1¼ pounds beef rump, round or short ribs

1¼ pounds pork butt or shoulder

1¼ pounds onions

2 garlic cloves

3 tablespoons lard

¼ cup sweet paprika

3 to 4 tablespoons hot paprika

3 cups (about) water

Salt and freshly ground black pepper

4 sprigs marjoram

2 sprigs thyme

1 to 2 bay leaves

¾ teaspoon caraway seed

1 to 2 dried chili peppers (optional)

4 tomatoes

1 large green bell pepper

1 large red bell pepper

½ cup full-bodied dry red wine

¼ cup tomato paste

Cayenne pepper

Pinch of sugar

6 servings
970 calories per serving
Preparation time: about 3½ hours

Wipe meat with a damp towel and pat thoroughly dry with paper towels.

- Trim fat from meat; chop fat finely and set aside. Cut lean, boneless meat into ¾-inch pieces.
- Chop onions coarsely and garlic finely.
- Place chopped fat in large saucepan or Dutch oven and render over moderate heat. Discard solid remnants. Add 1 tablespoon lard to saucepan.

- Increase heat and add meat and a bit more lard to saucepan in batches, browning well on all sides. Keep batches small so that meat browns quickly and juices are sealed in; if juices cook out meat will lose flavor and toughen. As each batch cooks, transfer to sieve set over bowl to drain. (Removing batches as they are done assures that meat will not overcook and dry out; draining meat in sieve enables you to capture juices without allowing meat fibers to soak up excess.)
- When all meat is cooked, melt remaining lard in same saucepan, add onions and sauté. After a few minutes add garlic and continue to cook until both are translucent.

- Return meat to saucepan and heat, stirring. Stir in both types of paprika and cook gently (paprika will taste bitter if it burns).
- Pour in water and drained meat juices. Season with salt, pepper, rinsed and dried marjoram and thyme sprigs, bay leaves and caraway. Reduce heat to low.
- Add chili pepper(s), if desired; remove seeds first so that goulash is not too hot.
- Cover goulash and simmer very gently for about 2½ hours.

- Cut crosswise slash in each tomato. Place in heatproof bowl, pour in boiling water to cover and let stand 1 to 2 minutes. Remove tomatoes and plunge into cold water; peel. Quarter tomatoes, remove stem and seeds and coarsely chop flesh.

- Halve bell peppers lengthwise; remove stems, seeds and membranes. Cut each pepper half into quarters lengthwise, then cut crosswise into narrow strips.
- Near end of cooking time add tomato and pepper pieces to goulash. Mix wine and tomato paste and blend in. Cook uncovered over low heat 30 more minutes; season with cayenne, sugar and salt. Serve goulash with *spaetzle*, boiled potatoes or bread, and a green salad.

Variation:
Goulash Szeged Style

This is made with equal weights of lean pork and coarse sauerkraut. Stir in sour cream to taste shortly before serving.

You can't really make an inauthentic goulash, for there's no such thing as *the* recipe. There are more than 20 classic variants of the dish; some use only beef, pork, veal or lamb, while others mix all sorts of meats. Even venison and fish goulashes are not unknown. In its native Hungary, goulash is an everyday dish made with whatever ingredients are at hand. Only onions, garlic and paprika, always readily available, are indispensable.

Braised Beef Roulades

The filling is what makes the dish here.

3 to 4 ounces bacon
2 sour pickles (3 to 4 ounces)
1 onion
4 beef roulades (about 5 ounces each), cut from round or flank
1 tablespoon sharp mustard
Salt and freshly ground black pepper
2 tablespoons vegetable oil
1½ cups meat broth
1 cup crème fraîche or sour cream

4 servings
670 calories per serving
Preparation time: about 2 hours

Refrigerate bacon for 30 minutes to firm. Blot pickles thoroughly dry.

- Slice bacon, if necessary, then cut into thin strips. Halve onion and slice thinly crosswise, starting at root end. Slice pickles, then cut into thin strips.
- Pat meat dry with paper towels and flatten with balls of thumbs; do not use a mallet, which will crush the delicate fibers.

- Spread meat thinly with mustard; season with salt and pepper. Distribute bacon, onion and pickle evenly over meat. Starting at narrow end, roll up meat, folding in long sides, to enclose filling completely.

- Secure each roll by inserting a skewer diagonally through both outer layers of meat, or tie with kitchen twine. Season with salt and pepper.
- Add oil to deep skillet large enough to hold roulades in a single layer. Place over high heat until very hot. Brown rolls well on all sides; if meat is cooked until brown and crusty, juices will not escape during braising and meat will remain tender and moist.

- Pour broth into skillet and scrape up browned bits from bottom with wooden spatula. Cover and cook over low heat about 1½ hours; liquid should simmer gently, never boil, as this will make meat tough and dry. Lift roulades out of skillet and remove skewers or twine; keep rolls warm.
- Bring braising liquid to boil and whisk in crème fraîche. Cook sauce uncovered over medium heat, stirring, until reduced to desired consistency.

- Pour sauce over roulades and serve with boiled potatoes or *spaetzle* and a vegetable side dish.

Variation: Beef Roulades with Feta Cheese

Prepare 4 beef roulades, about 5 ounces each, as above. Thinly slice 2 garlic cloves. Crumble 5 ounces feta cheese; coarsely chop 2 ounces blanched pistachios. Rinse 2 ounces (about ⅓ cup) dried currants; blot dry in kitchen towel. Divide these ingredients evenly among pieces of meat. Place 2 pitted black olives on each roulade. Roll up and secure meat as in master recipe. Brown well on all sides in 2 tablespoons oil. Pour 1 cup dry red wine and ½ cup water into skillet and scrape up browned bits from bottom. Add 1 teaspoon fresh thyme leaves, cover and braise roulades for 1½ hours.

Variation: Veal Birds

Gently flatten 4 thin veal scallops (about 3½ ounces each). Season with black pepper and spread thinly with herb-flavored mustard. Place 1 very thin slice of prosciutto or Westphalian ham and 1 shelled hard-cooked egg on each veal scallop. Roll up and secure meat as in master recipe. Lightly coat veal rolls in about 1 tablespoon all-purpose flour. Brown well on all sides in mixture of 1 tablespoon each butter and oil. Pour 1 cup hot chicken broth and ½ cup dry white wine into skillet and scrape up browned bits from bottom. Cover and braise veal birds over low heat for 25 minutes. Flavor sauce with fresh lemon juice, capers and herbed mustard.

The filling for meat rolls should always contain some fat—for example, in the form of bacon, ham or cheese—to keep the lean meat wrapper tender and juicy. Suitable meats for roulades include beef, veal, pork and turkey. Good-quality roulade meat is lean and free of gristle or sinew; meat containing too much connective tissue is likely to split or burst open during cooking. Choose beef top or bottom round, veal round or rump, or port butt slices.

Tournedos in Morel Cream Sauce

A choice dish that is very little work to prepare.

Tournedos are cut from the thinner part of the filet, and so are somewhat smaller than filet steaks. Morels, after truffles the most prized of all edible fungi (and therefore quite expensive), are available in dried form in gourmet specialty shops. You may substitute dried cèpes or porcini if you wish.

2 packets (about 10 grams each) dried morels
1 cup water
8 tournedos, about 3 ounces each
2 shallots
2 tablespoons vegetable oil
3 tablespoons butter
2 to 3 tablespoons dry white wine
1½ tablespoons Cognac
1 cup crème fraîche or sour cream
2 teaspoons chilled butter
1 heaping tablespoon whipped cream
Salt and freshly ground white pepper

4 servings
480 calories per serving
Preparation time: about 30 minutes
Soaking time: 6 hours

Cover mushrooms with 1 cup water and let stand 6 hours to soften. (Do not wash mushrooms before soaking; this will weaken their flavor.)
• Remove mushrooms from soaking water with slotted spoon. Transfer to strainer and rinse well under cold running water, shaking strainer to reach all sides of mushrooms; be sure to remove all traces of grit from crevices in the mushroom caps.

• Pour soaking water through coffee filter to remove all particles; set aside.
• Tie around circumference of each tournedo with kitchen twine so that they retain round shape during cooking. Mince shallots.
• Heat oil in skillet over high heat. Reduce heat to medium and add 1 tablespoon butter; melt, but do not brown.
• Add tournedos to skillet and brown on both sides for a total of 3 to 4 minutes, depending on whether you prefer meat very rare or medium rare. Remove tournedos from skillet and snip off twine. Wrap in foil and keep warm.
• Pour off all but a thin film of fat from skillet. Add remaining butter and heat well. Add shallot and stir over medium heat until translucent. Add morels and cook 1 minute, stirring.
• Pour wine and Cognac into skillet and scrape up browned bits from bottom with wooden spatula. Raise heat as high as possible and add mushroom soaking water and crème fraîche alternately in several additions. Boil down sauce, stirring constantly, until thick and creamy.
• Cut chilled butter into small bits and whisk into sauce. Stir in whipped cream. Season sauce with salt and pepper to taste.
• Place tournedos on heated serving places and surround with morel sauce. Serve immediately with rice.

Rump Steaks with Tomato Sauce

For those who have little time to spend at the stove but want to eat well nevertheless.

Rump steaks are ⅜- to ½-inch-thick slices cut from the rump roast. High-quality meat should be well marbled—that is, veined with thin streaks of fat and edged with a layer of fat about the thickness of a finger. Rump steaks taste best if cooked just to rare or medium rare.

1 pound, 10 ounces ripe tomatoes

1 large onion

4 garlic cloves

4 beef rump steaks (about 6 ounces each)

2 tablespoons olive oil

Salt and freshly ground black pepper

1 tablespoon drained capers

½ teaspoon dried oregano

4 servings
520 calories per serving
Preparation time: about 30 minutes

Blanch tomatoes in boiling water for 30 seconds. Plunge into cold water to stop cooking process; drain. Stem, peel, seed and dice tomatoes. Finely chop onion and garlic.

• Pat steaks dry with paper towels. Slash outer layer of fat at ¾-inch intervals just deeply enough to cut through membrane separating fat from meat; this membrane contracts during cooking, and if not cut it will cause steaks to curve.

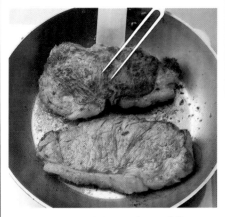

• Heat olive oil in heavy large skillet over high heat. Add steaks and cook 1 minute per side.

• Reduce heat and cook steaks, turning once, to desired doneness, 3 to 5 minutes. Transfer steaks to heated platter, season with salt and pepper and keep warm.

• Add onion and garlic to skillet and cook until translucent. Stir in tomato, cover and cook over medium heat 5 minutes. Add capers and oregano and season sauce to taste with salt and pepper. Serve steaks with sauce; accompany with French or Italian bread.

Roast Beef with Béarnaise Sauce

Perfect for large family gatherings.

1 beef roast with outer layer of fat (about 4½ pounds)

Freshly ground black pepper

2 shallots

4 white peppercorns

½ ounce mixed fresh tarragon and chervil stems

6 tablespoons dry white wine

¼ cup tarragon vinegar

1 cup (2 sticks) butter

3 egg yolks

3 tablespoons hot water

1 tablespoon finely chopped fresh tarragon leaves

1½ teaspoons finely chopped fresh chervil leaves

Salt

Cayenne pepper

10 servings
600 calories per serving
Preparation time: about 1 hour

Wipe meat with damp cloth and pat thoroughly dry; if meat is moist it will not brown properly and will lose juices.

• Adjust oven rack to lowest position and preheat oven to 475°F.

• Cut away half of fat layer covering meat. Score remaining fat into diamonds with sharp knife; do not cut into meat itself. Sprinkle all sides of meat generously with pepper, cover with foil and let stand 10 minutes.

• Insert meat thermometer into thickest part of roast; if roast is not very thick, insert thermometer diagonally (the stem should be completely surrounded with meat, or it will register oven temperature rather than internal temperature of roast). Be sure that face of thermometer is positioned so it will be easy to read during roasting. Place meat on roasting rack fat side up. Set rack into roasting pan and place in oven.

• Roast 20 minutes, then reduce oven temperature to 400°F. Meat will be fully cooked in another 20 to 30 minutes; roast to an internal temperature of about 113°F for very rare, about 131°F for medium rare.

• While meat cooks, prepare béarnaise sauce. Mince shallots. Crush peppercorns using mortar and pestle. Rinse and dry tarragon and chervil stems; chop coarsely.

• Combine wine, tarragon vinegar, shallot, pepper and herb stems in nonaluminum saucepan and bring to boil. Stir over medium heat until liquid is reduced to about 1 tablespoon. Pour reduced liquid through fine sieve, pressing on shallots and herbs with wooden spoon to extract all liquid. Keep liquid warm.

• Melt butter in clean saucepan over low heat; do not let butter brown. Skim off white foam and carefully pour clarified butter into another saucepan, leaving behind the milk solids in bottom of pan. Keep clarified butter warm but not too hot; if overheated it will curdle the egg yolks.

• Pour an inch or two of water into another saucepan and keep hot over low heat.

• Combine egg yolks and 3 tablespoons hot water in metal bowl and place over water in saucepan. Whisk until thick and foamy; keep water bath hot but *do not* let it boil.

• Whisk warm butter into yolks first by teaspoons, then in a thin stream.

• Whisk in reduced wine mixture by teaspoons. Blend in chopped herbs. Season sauce with salt and cayenne and keep warm.

• Remove thermometer from meat, wrap meat tightly in foil and let rest 15 minutes; during roasting the juices will have collected at the center of the meat, and the resting period allows them to redistribute throughout the roast.

• Slice roast across the grain. Season with salt and pepper. Pass sauce separately. Accompany roast with French or Italian bread.

The bigger the roast, the better the result—so goes the kitchen axiom. But don't be timid about fixing roast beef for a small group. Leftovers are delicious the next day, served cold and thinly sliced with a crisp salad. Roast beef should always be served on the rare side, never cooked through, or its aroma and flavor will be lost. Needless to say, success depends mainly on the quality of the meat. It must be well marbled, with a goodly layer of fat covering the top surface.

Filet Steaks Café de Paris

A classic preparation for which you will have to do a bit of advance planning.

1 shallot
1 anchovy fillet
1½ teaspoons drained capers
1½ teaspoons tomato paste
1½ teaspoons herb-flavored mustard
1½ teaspoons fresh lemon juice
1 tablespoon Cognac
3 dashes of Worcestershire sauce
¾ teaspoon sweet paprika
Pinch of curry powder
Pinch of cayenne pepper
Freshly ground black pepper
1½ teaspoons *herbes de Provence*
1 teaspoon chopped fresh parsley
Salt
7 tablespoons softened butter
1 teaspoon all-purpose flour
1 cup heavy cream
4 beef filet steaks, about 1¼ inches thick
3 tablespoons vegetable oil

4 servings
710 calories per serving
Preparation time: about 45 minutes
Resting time: 24 hours

For sauce, chop shallot so finely that it is reduced to a paste. Mince anchovy and capers.

• In small glass, ceramic or stainless steel bowl combine shallot, anchovy, capers, tomato paste, mustard, lemon juice, Cognac, Worcestershire, spices, herbs and salt to taste. Cover and let sauce base stand at room temperature 24 hours (the fermentation process that takes place will heighten the sauce's flavor).

• The next day, knead 1 teaspoon of the butter with flour; set aside. Whisk remaining butter into sauce base to make a smooth herb butter.

• Pour cream into saucepan and bring to boil. Whisk in flour-butter paste and return to boil. Remove from heat.

• Let cream cool somewhat; it should be just warm enough to melt herb butter (if hotter, the cream may curdle when the herb butter is added). Add herb butter to cream and whisk vigorously until completely absorbed; sauce will be thick enough to coat the back of a wooden spoon. Keep sauce warm, but do not cover with pan lid or condensed steam will drip back into sauce and spoil it.

• Flatten steaks somewhat with the balls of your thumbs. Pat steaks dry with paper towels.

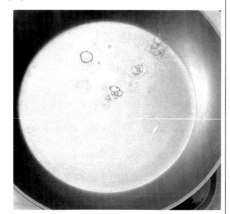

• Heat ungreased heavy skillet until a drop of water sprinkled onto the bottom sizzles and evaporates. Add oil and heat until tiny bubbles rise to surface.

• Add steaks to skillet and brown well on both sides over high heat; the meat must form a brown crust quickly to seal in juices. (Do not salt meat before cooking; salt will draw out juices and toughen meat.) As soon as steaks are well browned, reduce heat to medium and continue cooking to desired doneness.

• Transfer steaks to heated serving plates and season with salt and freshly ground pepper. Pour sauce around steaks and serve immediately.

• There are general rules about the cooking time for steaks, which will vary depending on the temperature and thickness of the meat. The quality of the steak is also important; pink, unaged meat will require longer cooking to become tender, and poor-quality steak will not cook to tenderness at all.

• For very rare, cook a filet steak of the given thickness for 1 minute over high heat, then 2 to 3 minutes per side over medium heat. The outside will be browned; inside, the meat is still uncooked.

• For rare, cook each side 3 minutes after the initial browning. The outside should be brown and crusty, the next layer of meat pink, and the center deep red.

• For medium, cook each side 6 minutes after initial browning. The center remains pink, but the outer layers are dark brown. Meat juices will run almost clear when steak is sliced.

Unfortunately, steaks are often thought of as a quick meal that takes no bother. For this reason, all manner of chancy cuts tend to wind up on the plate in place of the really tender meat that is required for good results. Since a properly cooked steak is a true delicacy—and needless to say is not inexpensive—we're offering this recipe. If you are short on time, serve a simple herb butter in place of the sauce (the recipe for which is from the Café de Paris in Monaco). Always be careful about the quality of the meat; buy it from a butcher you trust, not from the supermarket.

Boiled Beef with Chive Sauce

This must cook very slowly if it is to remain tender and juicy.

The best beef for boiling is cut from the rump. Some other cuts, such as brisket and bottom round, are also suitable. Don't remove the layer of fat until after the meat is cooked. Remember that "boiled" beef is really a misnomer: the meat must poach at the gentlest simmer, never actually boil.

4 beef marrow bones
2 quarts cold water
3¼ pounds boiling beef in one piece
1 piece (about 5 ounces) celery root
1 carrot
1 small leek
1 sprig parsley
1 onion
½ bunch parsley
2 bay leaves
8 black peppercorns
Salt
4 slices white bread, crusts removed
½ cup milk
2 hard-cooked egg yolks
2 raw egg yolks
½ cup vegetable oil
2 tablespoons fresh lemon juice
Freshly ground white pepper
2 bunches chives

6 servings
510 calories per serving
Preparation time: about 4¼ hours

Place marrow bones in saucepan or Dutch oven just large enough to hold bones and meat comfortably. Pour in water.

• Simmer bones gently for 30 minutes over medium-low heat. Do not skim foam; the protein particles it contains will help to clarify broth.

• Add meat to saucepan and reduce heat. (The meat must cook at below the boil, or broth will be cloudy and meat will be tough and dry. Adjust heat so that tiny bubbles rise to surface from bottom of saucepan.) Cover saucepan halfway and cook meat 1 hour, replenishing liquid with hot water as necessary to keep meat and bones covered.

• Meanwhile, peel celery root and carrot; wash leek and parsley sprig. Chop coarsely. Halve and peel onion. Add vegetables to broth with washed parsley, bay leaves and peppercorns; season with salt to taste. Cook another 2 to 2½ hours.

• While meat cooks, soak bread in milk until soft, then mash finely with fork. Beat until smooth with cooked and raw egg yolks. Beat in oil first a few drops at a

time, then a teaspoon at a time as though you were preparing mayonnaise. Beat in 2 tablespoons meat broth and lemon juice; season with salt and white pepper. Snip chives finely and stir into sauce.

• Remove meat from broth and cut against the grain into finger-thick slices. Pour a little broth over meat and serve with sauce. Freshly grated horseradish and boiled potatoes are perfect accompaniments.

Pot-Roasted Rib Steak with Vegetables

One of the choicest of beef cuts, the rib steak is admirably suited to slow pot roasting. It is important not to add the meat until the broth comes to a boil, so that the pores will be sealed immediately.

Gentle simmering in wine and broth makes the meat wonderfully flavorful.

1 quart meat broth
½ bottle (1½ cups) dry white wine
1 bay leaf
2 whole cloves
¾ teaspoon black peppercorns
1 onion
1 garlic clove
½ bunch parsley
1 beef rib steak, 2½ to 2¾ pounds
Salt
4 celery stalks
9 ounces carrots
2 parsley roots
1 leek
9 ounces sugar-snap or snow peas
2 tomatoes
¼ cup crème fraîche or sour cream

4 servings
760 calories per serving
Preparation time: about 1¼ hours

C ombine broth, wine, bay leaf, cloves and peppercorns in Dutch oven and bring to boil.
• Halve onion. Add to broth mixture with peeled whole garlic clove, washed parsley and meat. Cover and return to boil over high heat, then reduce heat, season with salt and simmer gently, half covered, for 1½ hours.

• Wash and trim celery, carrots, parsley roots and leek. Remove tough strings from celery and chop stalks coarsely. Trim carrot tops, leaving about ¼ inch of green. Peel parsley roots. Coarsely chop leek. Remove strings from pea pods. Pour boiling water over tomatoes; plunge into ice water. Peel, stem, seed and chop tomatoes.
• Add celery, carrots, parsley roots, leek and peas to Dutch oven about 20 minutes before end of cooking time. Add tomatoes and cook 2 more minutes.
• Transfer meat to heated platter and surround with vegetables.
• Remove 1 cup broth and whisk together with crème fraîche. Pour over meat and serve immediately.

Beef Stroganoff

Not inexpensive, but quickly prepared.

1¼ pounds beef tenderloin
1 small onion (4 ounces)
7 to 8 ounces mushrooms
1 tablespoon vegetable oil
3 tablespoons butter
Salt and freshly ground black pepper
2 to 3 teaspoons prepared mustard
1⅓ cups crème fraîche or sour cream
1½ teaspoons meat extract, such as Bovril
1 tablespoon fresh lemon juice

4 servings
550 calories per serving
Preparation time: about 30 minutes

Wipe meat with damp towel and carefully trim away all fat, membrane and gristle.

• Cut meat into ⅜-inch-thick slices, then into ⅜-inch strips.

• Halve onion lengthwise. Place one half cut side down on cutting board and slice crosswise, then slice lengthwise at right angles to first cuts to form fine dice. Repeat with second half of onion.

• Clean and slice mushrooms.
• Heat ungreased heavy large skillet or saucepan until very hot. Add oil and heat, then add half of butter.

• Add meat in batches and stir with wooden spatula to seal pores of meat on all sides. As each batch cooks, transfer to strainer set over bowl to drain. When all meat is cooked, add remaining butter to skillet. Add onion and mushrooms and cook, stirring, until onion is translucent and mushrooms are soft.
• Season mushroom mixture with salt and pepper. Stir in mustard and cook briefly. Add a few drops of water and scrape up browned bits from bottom of pan.

• Stir crème fraîche with fork to loosen. Pour into pan and stir to blend; if necessary, cook to thicken slightly. Stir in meat extract and lemon juice for a piquant taste.
• Season meat with salt and pepper; stir into sauce. Heat through over a gentle flame, stirring; do not cook meat further or it may toughen.

• Stir in juices drained from meat to finish sauce.
• Serve immediately; the Stroganoff will not be nearly as good if it has to wait. Accompany with a green salad and parsley potatoes or buttered vegetables; instead of parsley potatoes you might prefer rice, hash-browned or *rösti* potatoes, or French bread.

Variation: Veal *Geschnetzeltes*, Zurich-Style

Though this is actually an entirely different dish, its preparation very much resembles that of beef Stroganoff. Cut 1¼ pounds veal tenderloin into slices about ³⁄₁₆ inch thick, then into strips no thicker than ³⁄₁₆ inch. Finely chop 2 to 3 onions. Heat 1 tablespoon vegetable oil and 1 generous tablespoon butter in large skillet; add meat and cook in batches. As each batch cooks, transfer to strainer set over bowl to drain. Pour off cooking fat and melt 2 tablespoons fresh butter in same skillet. Add onion and cook until translucent, then sprinkle with 1 to 2 tablespoons all-purpose flour, stir through and cook briefly. Pour in ½ cup rich stock or broth and scrape up browned bits from bottom of skillet. Add ½ cup dry white wine and bring to vigorous boil. Season with salt and pepper. Reduce heat and stir in ½ cup heavy cream; do not boil or cream will curdle. Return meat to skillet and heat through, being careful not to boil. Pour in juices drained from veal. Serve immediately, garnished with chopped fresh parsley. *Rösti* potatoes make a delicious side dish.

Beef tenderloin, onions, and crème fraîche or sour cream are the key ingredients in beef Stroganoff. The mushrooms are not an absolute must, but they do lend rich flavor. Sometimes chopped pickles or tomatoes, even beet or potato slices find their way into a Stroganoff.

Braised Marinated Shoulder Roast

The aroma of the marinade penetrates through and through the meat.

If you don't grow lemon balm in your own garden, try a nursery. The herb, a member of the mint family, has a strong clean lemon aroma.

| 4½ pounds boneless veal or pork shoulder, in one piece |
| Freshly ground white pepper |
| 2 onions |
| 2 garlic cloves |
| 4 sprigs thyme |
| 2 sprigs sage |
| 2 bay leaves |
| 1 lemon |
| 1½ cups full-bodied dry white wine |
| 6 tablespoons cold-pressed olive oil |
| Salt |
| ½ cup hot meat broth |
| 1 bunch lemon balm, chopped |
| 2 to 3 tablespoons drained capers |
| Salt and freshly ground black pepper |

6 servings
675 calories per serving
Marinating time: at least 24 hours
Preparation time: about 3 to 3½ hours

Wipe veal or pork shoulder with damp towel. Sprinkle generously with white pepper and rub into meat.
• Slice onions into thin rings; chop garlic. Combine in mixing bowl.
• Rinse fresh herbs and shake dry. Add to onion mixture with bay leaves.

• Scrub lemon under hot running water; dry. Cut off a paper-thin strip of peel (colored part only) about 1¼ inches long; cut piece of peel in half. Reserve lemon.
• Place meat in plastic bag just large enough to hold it comfortably. Spread onion-herb mixture around meat, adding pieces of lemon peel. Pour in wine and 4 tablespoons olive oil. Seal bag tightly and shake several times to ensure that meat is evenly coated with marinade. Set meat in a cool place (or refrigerate) to marinate

at least 24 hours, preferably 1½ to 2 days, shaking bag occasionally.
• Remove meat from marinade and drain, reserving marinade. Dry meat well all over.

• Season meat with salt and rub in carefully.
• Heat remaining 2 tablespoons olive oil in roasting pan or Dutch oven over high heat. Add veal and brown well on all sides. Add some liquid from marinade and scrape up browned bits from bottom of pan. As soon as liquid comes to boil, add remaining marinade (with solids) and meat broth; return to boil. Cover and braise over medium heat for 2 to 2½ hours.

• Baste meat with braising liquid from time to time to keep veal moist and help seasoning penetrate.
• Remove meat; cover or wrap in aluminum foil and keep warm.
• Strain braising liquid into saucepan and boil rapidly until reduced and thickened. Degrease.
• Cut 1 or 2 more paper-thin strips of lemon peel, leaving behind any white membrane. Cut peel into very fine julienne. Squeeze juice from part or all of lemon.

• As soon as sauce has reached desired consistency, stir in lemon juice to taste, julienned peel, lemon balm and capers. Cook sauce gently for a few more minutes; do not boil. Season with salt and pepper and pour into sauceboat or serving bowl.
• Slice meat against the grain. To serve, garnish with fresh herbs if desired; accompany with buttered vegetables and noodles or boiled potatoes.

Variation: Braised Marinated Leg of Lamb

A small (about 4½-pound) leg of lamb can be marinated and braised according to this recipe. The preparation is exactly the same, but the herbs can be varied if you wish: rosemary and oregano are particularly tasty with lamb, and dill is good instead of lemon balm. With this dish it is convenient to cook boiling potatoes along with the meat in the braising liquid; peel them, cut into equal-size chunks and allow about 45 minutes to an hour cooking time. Remove potatoes with the meat and keep warm while you prepare sauce. Heavy cream or crème fraîche makes a delicious addition to the sauce.

Even though it is exceptionally lean and tender, many people shy away from veal for large roasts because they don't think it has a pronounced enough flavor. You won't find this to be the case here: Herbs, garlic, wine and olive oil make for juicy, full-flavored meat. Though most cooks choose veal leg for braising, this marinating treatment is particularly good for more economical veal shoulder. Since it has little fat or sinew, it turns out very lean and tender, and it is nicely complemented by a full-flavored sauce.

Frikadellen (Sautéed Meatballs)

Easy and versatile.

These can be made from beef, pork, veal and lamb, and flavored with red peppers, capers, dill or curry; sometimes the meatballs are also stuffed with cheese, olives or egg. Fry a test meatball before cooking the whole batch; if it doesn't hold together well, try adding breadcrumbs or egg yolk.

1 stale dinner roll
1 cup (about) lukewarm water
1 onion
1 garlic clove
1 to 2 anchovy fillets
½ bunch parsley
½ bunch chives
1 generous pound mixed ground meat
1 egg
1½ teaspoons sweet paprika
Salt and freshly ground black pepper
2 tablespoons vegetable oil
1 generous tablespoon butter

4 servings
380 calories per serving
Preparation time: about 30 minutes

Break or chop roll into large pieces, pour lukewarm water over and set aside to soften.
- Meanwhile, mince onion and garlic. Blot anchovy fillets dry (if you are using anchovies packed in salt, first rinse briefly with cold water). Mince anchovies or crush in mortar. Rinse parsley and chives and shake dry; finely chop parsley, finely snip chives.
- Squeeze bread dry and combine in bowl with onion, garlic, anchovy and herbs. Add meat, egg and paprika; season generously with salt and pepper.

- Combine all ingredients well with fork, using a light hand and drawing the fork through the mixture from top to bottom as though folding with a rubber spatula. (Ingredients can also be blended with your hands, if you prefer.)

- Dipping hands in cold water, form 8 equal meatballs; flatten slightly.
- Heat large skillet. Add oil; when oil is hot, add butter and allow to melt.
- Arrange meatballs in skillet and sauté over high heat until well browned on both sides. Reduce heat to medium and cook meatballs another 5 minutes on both sides.
- Remove from skillet and drain briefly. Serve very hot or let cool before serving. When hot, *Frikadellen* are good with a mixed salad, green beans with bacon, or buttered vegetables and boiled potatoes. Potato salad is the ideal accompaniment if meatballs are served cold.

Stuffed Meat Loaf

Every cook seems to have his or her own variation on meat loaf. Some stuff it with hard-cooked eggs, others with blanched leeks. Try this version too, which is tempting for both its savory aroma and its attractive appearance.

Proof that a feast doesn't have to be expensive.

1½ stale dinner rolls
1½ cups warm water
2 small onions
1 to 2 garlic cloves
2 dill pickles
1 to 2 tablespoons drained capers
2 eggs
Juice of ½ lemon
1¼ pounds mixed ground meat
Salt and freshly ground black pepper
Cayenne pepper
2 small, elongated bell peppers
1 bunch chives
2 bunches herbs (basil, dill, parsley)
3 tablespoons butter
½ cup hot meat broth
½ cup heavy cream
1 tablespoon sour cream
Sweet paprika

4 servings
670 calories per serving
Preparation time: about 1½ hours

S oak roll in warm water until softened. Finely chop onions, garlic, pickles.
• Squeeze roll dry and combine with onion, garlic, pickle, capers, eggs, lemon juice and meat. Mix thoroughly. Season with salt, pepper, cayenne.
• Core and seed peppers. Chop pepper and mix into ¾ of meat.

• Chop herbs finely. Mix into remaining ¼ of meat; stuff peppers with mixture.
• Adjust oven rack to second position from bottom and preheat oven to 400°F.
• Form larger portion of meat into loaf around peppers.
• Oil baking pan large enough to hold meat loaf. Transfer loaf to pan and bake 30 minutes, spreading often with butter.
• Whisk together meat broth, cream, sour cream and paprika. Pour over meat loaf and bake 10 more minutes.
• Transfer loaf to serving platter and surround with sauce. Serve immediately.

Roast Leg of Lamb

A true celebration dish.

1 small leg of lamb, about 2¼ pounds
5 garlic cloves
2 juniper berries
¾ teaspoon black peppercorns
¼ cup cold-pressed olive oil
2 tablespoons gin
2 sprigs rosemary
2 bay leaves
3 tablespoons butter
Salt

4 servings
650 calories per serving
Preparation time: about 1 hour
Marinating time: about 24 hours

Wipe lamb with damp towel and pat thoroughly dry.
• Finely dice or chop garlic.
• Place juniper berries and peppercorns in a small mound on cutting board or work surface and rest the side of a wide, sturdy knife blade on top.

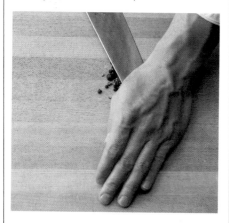

• Press down hard on blade to crush spices; if necessary, chop spices as well to reduce to tiny bits. (A mortar and pestle can be used if you wish, but it is not really necessary for such a small quantity.)
• Combine garlic and crushed spices in a small bowl or cup, add olive oil and gin and blend to a smooth paste.
• Rinse rosemary and shake dry; strip leaves from stem. Chop leaves coarsely.
• Lay a large sheet of double-strength aluminum foil on work surface. Sprinkle half of rosemary in center of foil.
• Crumble bay leaves between the palms of your hands; sprinkle half over rosemary.

• Spread lamb with garlic mixture on all sides and rub in thoroughly. Place meat on herb mixture and sprinkle with remaining rosemary and bay leaf pieces; rub herbs into meat. Close foil tightly around meat and let stand in a cool place or refrigerate for about 24 hours.
• About 4 hours before roasting, open foil and bring lamb to room temperature.
• Adjust oven rack to second position from bottom and preheat oven to 475°F.
• Discard foil. Using paper towel, wipe as much garlic mixture as possible from meat, as garlic burns easily and will cause a bitter taste.
• Melt butter in small saucepan; do not brown.

• Sprinkle lamb with salt all over. Place on rack in roasting pan and brush generously with part of butter. Immediately place in oven and reduce oven temperature to 425°F. Roast 25 to 30 minutes for rare, basting frequently with remaining butter and meat drippings.
• Remove lamb from oven, wrap in fresh sheet of foil and let rest 15 minutes.

• Unwrap lamb and place on cutting board, holding bone firmly. Starting at thickest part of meat and using a very sharp knife, thinly slice meat across grain and perpendicular to bone. Turn meat slightly after each cut to obtain even slices.
• If you would prefer not to carve meat with bone in, the individual muscles (which are clearly visible) can be separated from the bone and carved one by one, diagonally across or perpendicular to grain of meat; the slices will be of different sizes. Season slices lightly with salt and pepper if you wish. Spoon juices from roasting pan over meat and serve immediately. Garnish with fresh vegetables if desired. Roast lamb goes . particularly well with green beans with bacon, braised oyster mushrooms, or ratatouille, along with *rösti* potatoes, raw-potato home fries or potato-leek gratin (see Index for all these recipes).

Tip: If you use a meat thermometer—which is available at little cost in well-stocked housewares shops—it is easy to tell precisely when the meat is done. After brushing meat with butter, insert thermometer into thickest part, where it will not touch bone. Remove lamb from oven when it reaches desired temperature (about 125°F for rare, 135°F to 145°F for medium and 150°F to 155°F for medium well). Wrap in foil to rest. When you slide meat into oven, be sure thermometer is positioned so that you can read it easily.

The best roasts come from six-month- to one-year-old lamb; at this age the meat has developed full flavor, but the fat is still soft and thin. Nice young lamb is recognizable by its light red meat and white fat, which is easily separated from the flesh. Lamb should always be roasted rare, never browned through. Remember, too, that it must always rest for a little while before slicing so that the juices distribute themselves through the meat and do not run out during carving.

Marinated Lamb Chops

Nowadays lamb is becoming more common in the supermarkets, with both American and New Zealand types available. No matter where the meat is from, lamb harmonizes beautifully with fresh herbs.

These are luscious when cooked rare and served hot.

4 double lamp chops, each about 6 ounces and ¾ inch thick

3 garlic cloves

1 bunch parsley

3 sprigs thyme

2 tablespoons Cognac

1 lemon

Freshly ground black pepper

¼ cup olive oil

Salt

4 servings
660 calories per serving
Preparation time: about 30 minutes
Marinating time: at least 4 hours

Wipe chops with damp towel to remove any particles of bone. Blot meat dry with paper towels.

• Using a very sharp knife, carefully slash layer of fat and membrane around each chop at ¾-inch intervals; do not cut into meat, or juices will run out and lamb will be dry.

• Mince or press garlic. Rinse parsley and thyme and shake dry; mince both herbs. Mix garlic, herbs and Cognac to a smooth paste.
• Scrub lemon under hot water and dry well. Grate a bit of lemon peel, then halve fruit and squeeze out juice. Combine grated peel and juice with herb paste and season generously with pepper. Whisk in about 3 tablespoons olive oil a drop or two at a time.

• Spread both sides of lamb chops with herb mixture, place chops in bowl and pour remaining marinade over. Cover tightly with foil and let stand at least 4 hours in a cool place, but preferably not in refrigerator.
• If you must marinate lamb in refrigerator, remove it about 1 hour before cooking so meat reaches room temperature.
• Heat ungreased heavy large skillet until very hot, then add remaining olive oil and heat well. Add chops (with marinade) and brown thoroughly over high heat for 1 to 2 minutes per side. Reduce heat to medium-low and cook another 2 to 3 minutes, depending on doneness you prefer.
• Remove meat from skillet and blot off excess fat with paper towels. Season both sides with salt and, if desired, pepper. Serve immediately; lamb is best when very hot. This dish is very good with green beans with bacon (see Index) or a mixed salad , plus raw-potato home fries or French bread.

Oven-Braised Lamb Chops with Vegetables

Lamb is wonderfully tender when braised gently with lots of vegetables and herbs. Bring this dish to the table as hot as possible for best flavor. Instead of leg chops you may use thriftier shoulder chops or neck slices.

A perfect fall dinner, this is light and savory with fresh herbs.

1 generous pound baking potatoes
2 onions
3 garlic cloves
1 bunch soup greens
1 generous pound tomatoes
8 lamb leg chops, about 5 ounces each
Salt and freshly ground black pepper
¼ cup all-purpose flour
½ cup olive oil
1 cup dry red wine
½ cup meat broth
3 sprigs thyme
2 sprigs oregano
1 bay leaf
1 bunch basil, chopped
½ bunch parsley, chopped

4 servings
950 calories per serving
Preparation time: about 1½ hours

Peel and wash potatoes. Coarsely chop onions; finely chop garlic. Wash and chop soup greens. Blanch tomatoes in boiling water for 30 seconds. Plunge into cold water to stop cooking process; drain. Peel, stem, seed and dice tomatoes.

• Season lamb with salt and pepper and sift flour lightly over both sides. Tap off excess flour.
• Adjust oven rack to lowest position and preheat oven to 350°F.
• Heat ¼ cup olive oil in large flameproof casserole. Add lamb and brown on both sides. Remove and keep warm.
• Heat remaining olive oil. Sauté first onion, garlic and soup greens, then potatoes, turning to brown evenly.
• Arrange meat over vegetables in casserole. Pour in wine and broth. Spread tomatoes over meat. Add rinsed herb sprigs and bay leaf.
• Cover casserole and bake until meat is tender, 60 to 70 minutes.
• Serve sprinkled with basil and parsley.

Roast Chicken Stuffed with Scallion and Apple

The perfect combination of moist stuffing and crisp skin.

1 whole chicken, about 3 pounds (reserve liver, heart and gizzard)
1 bunch scallions
1 tart apple
½ lemon
3 tablespoons butter
½ bunch parsley, chopped
Salt and freshly ground white pepper
A few saffron threads
1 garlic clove

4 servings
470 calories per serving
Preparation time: about 1¾ hours

Rinse chicken well inside and out; dry thoroughly.
- Wash and dry scallions; trim root ends and tops, leaving about ¼ of green part. Slice into thin rings. Peel and quarter apple; remove core. Chop apple quarters.

- Remove peel (colored part only) from lemon half with sharp knife. Cut into fine julienne. Squeeze lemon and reserve juice.
- Finely chop chicken liver, heart and gizzard.
- Adjust oven rack to lowest position and preheat oven to 400°F.

- For stuffing, melt 1 tablespoon butter in large skillet; do not brown. Add scallions and apple and cook over medium heat, stirring, until translucent, about 3 minutes. Add lemon peel, chicken giblets and parsley and cook, stirring, until giblets turn grayish in color. Season with salt and white pepper and let cool to lukewarm.

- Season chicken inside and out with salt and white pepper and rub seasonings in well.
- Stuff chicken through tail end; do not pack stuffing tightly, as it will expand during cooking and may split skin of chicken.

- Secure opening of chicken with four toothpicks or skewers, inserting them horizontally through skin. Lace kitchen string through toothpicks and tie ends.
- Place chicken in roasting pan breast side up; pan should be large enough that chicken can be turned without difficulty. Place in oven.
- Melt remaining butter in saucepan; do not brown. Crumble saffron and add to butter.
- Force garlic through press into butter. Add lemon juice.

- Roast chicken about 1¼ hours, turning breast side down halfway through cooking time and basting frequently with garlic butter to make skin brown and crisp. Serve hot with potato croquettes or French bread and a mixed salad.

Variation: Grandma's Roast Chicken

Soak 4 slices firm white bread (crusts removed) in water; squeeze dry. Combine with 7 ounces finely chopped chicken livers, 1 chopped onion, 3 ounces chopped bacon and ¼ cup chopped fresh parsley. Mix in leaves from 2 thyme sprigs, ¼ cup heavy cream and 1 egg. Season stuffing with salt and freshly ground black pepper. Prepare 1 roasting chicken (about 3½ pounds) as above; season with salt and pepper. Stuff chicken and secure opening. Place in roaster with lid. Cover and roast on lowest rack of preheated 400°F oven 1 hour, basting frequently with melted butter. While chicken cooks, peel 1 generous pound boiling potatoes and 9 ounces shallots. Melt 7 tablespoons butter in large saucepan. Add 3 tablespoons sugar and stir until caramelized. Add potatoes and shallots and turn to coat all sides with sugar mixture. Pour in ½ cup meat broth. Season vegetables with salt and cook 15 minutes over low heat. Surround chicken with glazed vegetables and bake uncovered another 15 minutes to brown. Sprinkle with chopped parsley and serve.

Young, range-fed chickens have the most tender and flavorful meat; it will be worth your while to find a shop selling chickens that have roamed free rather than those raised indoors. Unfortunately, there is often no alternative to frozen chicken. If you use a frozen bird, thaw it slowly—that is, for at least 12 hours in the refrigerator—before cooking. For oven roasting use only young birds, around six months old. If you baste the chicken with seasoned butter you will get the crisp golden brown skin that everyone adores.

Coq au Vin

Nearly every French region has a different recipe for *coq au vin*, or chicken in wine sauce. One will replace Cognac with *eau de vie*, while another will omit the flambéing. Sometimes white wine is used instead of red, and there are versions that are heavily seasoned with garlic.

This is very good when made ahead and rewarmed before serving.

1 frying chicken, about 2¾ to 3 pounds
3 to 4 ounces bacon
3 onions
3 tablespoons vegetable oil
2 tablespoons (¼ stick) butter
Salt and freshly ground white pepper
1 tablespoon all-purpose flour
1 bunch parsley
2 sprigs thyme
3 tablespoons Cognac
2 cups full-bodied dry red wine
1 bay leaf
7 ounces pearl onions
1 pound fresh mushrooms
Juice of 1 lemon

4 servings
860 calories per serving
Preparation time: about 2 hours

Cut chicken into 8 serving pieces. Dice bacon and onions.
• Heat 2 tablespoons oil and 1 tablespoon butter in heavy large saucepan or flameproof casserole. Add bacon and cook over low heat until fat is rendered. Remove bacon with slotted spoon and set aside. Add onion and brown lightly in fat remaining in saucepan; remove and set aside. Add remaining tablespoon of oil to saucepan.
• Season chicken with salt and white pepper. Increase heat to medium-high, add chicken pieces to saucepan and brown on all sides. Sprinkle with flour and continue cooking until flour is browned. Return onion to saucepan.
• Adjust oven rack to lowest position and preheat oven to 350°F. Rinse fresh herbs.
• Warm Cognac over very low flame or in candle warmer. Ignite and pour into saucepan; flames will soon subside. Pour in red wine.
• Scrape up browned bits from bottom of pan. Add 2 parsley stems with thyme and bay leaf. Cover and bake 1 hour.
• Peel pearl onions.
• Melt remaining tablespoon of butter; add onions. Season with salt and pepper and sauté briefly to brown slightly. Reduce heat, cover and cook 20 minutes, or until tender but not soft.
• Toss mushrooms with lemon juice.
• Remove pearl onions from pan and set aside. Add mushrooms (with lemon

juice), season with salt and pepper and stew 5 minutes.
• Remove chicken parts from casserole and keep warm. Discard whole herbs.

• To degrease cooking liquid, lay several sheets of paper towel on surface one after the other, removing each as it becomes soaked with fat.
• Return chicken to sauce with bacon, pearl onions and mushrooms. Cover and bake 15 minutes longer. Sprinkle with remaining parsley, chopped. Serve.

Chicken Curry

This marvelous dish is easy to prepare, since the chicken simmers slowly without needing any attention. The most important thing here is the spice mixture; don't use commercial curry powder. All the necessary spices are available in well-stocked markets or spice shops.

A spicy-hot dish from classic Indian cuisine.

1 frying chicken, about 3 pounds
1 onion
1 to 2 garlic cloves
1 piece fresh ginger root, ¾ inch long
2 tablespoons vegetable oil
2 tablespoons (¼ stick) butter
1½ cups water
2½ teaspoons turmeric
1¼ teaspoons cumin
1¼ teaspoons mustard seed
1¼ teaspoons fennel seed
1 teaspoon crushed red pepper flakes
¾ teaspoon aniseed
¾ teaspoon ground coriander
5 cardamom seeds
1 piece cinnamon stick, about 1½ inches long
1 blade of mace, or ¼ teaspoon ground mace or freshly grated nutmeg
Salt
Juice of ½ lemon

4 servings
320 calories per serving
Preparation time: about 3½ hours

Rinse chicken inside and out with cold water; blot dry. Cut into 8 serving pieces.
• Chop onion and garlic. Peel ginger root, rinse and slice thinly.
• Heat oil and butter in large skillet. Add chicken parts and brown on all sides over high heat. Add onion, garlic and ginger and stir until onion is translucent.

• Pour in water and scrape up browned bits from bottom of skillet. Mix in spices and salt to taste. Cover skillet and cook gently over low heat, about 3 hours.
• The meat should be so well cooked that it can be easily loosened from the bones with a spoon.
• Stir in lemon juice. Serve curry hot with steamed rice.

Chicken Breast and Broccoli Stir-Fry

Eat this with chopsticks instead of knife and fork. *Sambal oelek* is an Indonesian spice available in specialty shops and Oriental markets.

2 tablespoons cornstarch

¼ cup soy sauce

3 tablespoons rice wine or dry Sherry

Freshly ground white pepper

2 whole chicken breasts, about 1 pound each

2¼ pounds broccoli

Salt

¼ cup sesame seed

¼ cup vegetable oil

1 cup chicken broth

Pinch of sugar

Juice of ½ lemon

Cayenne pepper

Sambal oelek

4 servings
465 calories per serving
Preparation time: about 45 minutes

C ombine cornstarch with a scant half of the soy sauce, 2 tablespoons wine or Sherry and pepper to taste in mixing bowl and whisk to blend.

- Skin chicken breasts; separate meat from bone by making a vertical cut immediately to either side of breastbone. Cut meat across the grain into very thin strips. Add to soy sauce mixture and turn to coat well on all sides. Let stand, covered, 15 to 20 minutes.
- Trim leaves from broccoli.

- Cut broccoli florets from stalks; cut florets into pieces as equal as possible in size so that they will cook evenly. Thinly peel stems of florets without removing tiny leaves. Peel large broccoli stems more thickly and cut into sticks.
- Drop broccoli florets and stems into large pot of rapidly boiling salted water and cook 4 minutes. Remove with skimmer or slotted spoon and immediately plunge into large bowl of ice water to stop cooking process; this will preserve the vegetable's fresh green color.
- When broccoli is completely cool, drain thoroughly in colander.

- Place ungreased large skillet over high heat until very hot. Add sesame seed and stir constantly until golden. Remove and set aside.
- Pour some of the oil into hot skillet and heat well. Lift chicken out of marinade, letting excess drain back into bowl.
- Add chicken to skillet in small batches and stir-fry over high heat until browned. As each batch is cooked, immediately transfer to colander or sieve set over bowl. Add more oil to pan as necessary.

- As soon as all chicken is cooked, pour remaining oil into skillet, add broccoli and stir-fry until cooked on all sides but not browned.

- Pour chicken broth into bowl with leftover marinade and blend well. Immediately stir into skillet with broccoli and cook over high heat 2 to 3 minutes.
- Add chicken strips and any collected juices. Stir just until heated through; do not cook further.
- Season with remaining soy sauce and wine, salt, pepper, sugar, lemon juice, and cayenne and *sambal oelek* to taste. Sprinkle with sesame seed and serve immediately with steamed rice or French bread.

Variation: Beef Tenderloin with Asparagus

Slice about 1 pound, 5 ounces beef tenderloin across grain, then cut into fine strips. Marinate as in above recipe. Meanwhile, peel bottom stalks of 2¼ pounds asparagus; snap off any woody parts. Cut stalks diagonally into 1-inch lengths. Drop into large pot of rapidly boiling salted water and blanch 2 to 3 minutes. Remove with skimmer or slotted spoon and plunge into ice water. Drain well. Stir-fry meat in batches, remove from skillet and add asparagus to skillet. Proceed according to master recipe, replacing sesame seed with blanched almond halves or flaked coconut, if you wish.

Variation: Stir-Fried Pork with Vegetables

This can be prepared with broccoli or asparagus exactly according to the master recipe. Use pork tenderloin or fresh ham.

Easy preparation, short cooking time and wholesome freshness distinguish this dish, borrowed from Oriental cooking. For best results remember three important things: the meat must be cooked quickly in small batches, the vegetable should retain its crispness, and once the liquid is added to the skillet the meat

must only be reheated, not cooked further. Give your imagination free rein with seasoning: minced garlic or julienned red pepper, for example, makes an excellent addition. The broccoli can be replaced with zucchini as well as asparagus.

Rare Filet of Venison

This is among the classics of European, particularly German, cuisine.

1 saddle of venison, about 3¼ pounds
2 ounces bacon
¼ cup vegetable oil
1 onion
1 garlic clove
1 carrot
1 small piece celery root (about 3½ ounces)
6 juniper berries
1 bay leaf
¾ teaspoon mustard seed
8 black peppercorns
1 whole clove
1 sprig rosemary
1½ tablespoons canned whole cranberry sauce
1 cup full-bodied dry red wine
1 heaping tablespoon all-purpose flour
2 tablespoons (¼ stick) butter
⅔ cup crème fraîche or sour cream
Salt and freshly ground black pepper
A few drops of fresh lemon juice
Pinch of cayenne pepper

4 servings
785 calories per serving
Preparation time: about 2 hours

If possible, ask your butcher to skin venison saddle and give you the trimmings. Wipe meat with damp towel to remove any bits of skin or bone. Blot meat thoroughly dry so that pores will seal quickly during cooking.

- Using a very sharp knife, remove small filets from under venison spine and large filets lying on ribs. Trim meat of any bits of skin or fat; reserve.

- Hack bones into fairly small pieces with cleaver; this is simplest if you first separate ribs from spine with one or two sharp blows.
- Finely dice bacon and place in large Dutch oven. Add about 1 tablespoon oil.
- Add bones and scraps of meat and fat. Cook, stirring frequently, until colored on all sides.
- Meanwhile, coarsely chop onion, garlic, carrot and peeled celery root. Add to pot and cook, stirring frequently, until lightly browned. Stir in juniper berries, bay leaf, mustard seed, peppercorns and clove. Rinse rosemary and shake dry; add to Dutch oven.

- Mix in cranberry sauce and a splash of wine; scrape up browned bits from bottom of pot with a wooden spatula.
- Bring mixture to boil over high heat, stirring frequently, and boil until liquid is evaporated. Add another generous splash of wine and again boil until evaporated.
- Sift flour over mixture through a small sieve. Stir and cook until flour is lightly browned, then add remaining wine and enough water almost to cover ingredients. Bring to boil over high heat, then reduce heat to medium, cover pot halfway and cook gently for 1 hour.

- Heat remaining oil in large skillet. Add butter and heat until melted and hot.

- Pat large venison filets dry and place in skillet, halving them crosswise if they are too long for the pan. Brown on all sides over medium heat, about 10 minutes.
- Pat small filets dry and brown for about 2 minutes.
- Wrap meat in foil and let rest about 15 minutes.
- Meanwhile, pour contents of Dutch oven through large strainer, pressing on solids to extract all juices.
- Pour strained liquid into saucepan and bring to boil. Whisk in crème fraîche and boil until sauce is creamy and reduced to desired consistency.
- Season sauce with salt, pepper, lemon juice and a hint of cayenne.

- Salt and pepper filets; cut into thick slices diagonally across grain. Pass sauce separately. Good side dishes are red cabbage or broccoli and *spaetzle* or boiled potatoes.

The traditional custom of larding venison saddle, marinating it for days and then cooking it for hours is no longer practiced either by chefs or by home cooks—this exceptionally tender, lean meat deserves better treatment! When cooked only in butter or in a mixture of butter and oil it retains all its flavor and juices. The resting time after cooking is very important, though; without it, the tender meat will weep its juices and dry out. The flavorful sauce is prepared ahead from venison bones and trimmings.

Rabbit Stew with Prunes

An unusual and delicious combination.

You can make this excellent dish with either domestic or wild rabbit. Ask your butcher to divide the rabbit up into legs, two back halves and the breast halves. Don't stint on the prunes; buy only pitted, unsulfured fruit of the best quality.

1 orange
14 ounces pitted prunes
3 scant tablespoons brandy
2 cups dry white wine
1 dressed rabbit, about 4½ pounds
3 to 4 ounces lean bacon
2 shallots
2 carrots
3 tablespoons vegetable oil
1 tablespoon butter
Salt and coarsely crushed white pepper
2 sprigs thyme
1 bay leaf
3 juniper berries
1 whole clove
1 piece cinnamon stick, about ¾ inch long
½ cup heavy cream

6 servings
860 calories per serving
Preparation time: about 1½ hours
Marinating time: 3 hours

Wash orange under hot running water and dry thoroughly. Remove about ¼ of peel (colored part only; the white pith underneath is bitter). Cut peel into fine julienne. Halve and squeeze orange.

• Rinse prunes briefly in cold water; pat dry with paper towels. Combine prunes and orange peel in mixing bowl and pour in orange juice and brandy. Add 1 cup white wine, cover and let stand 3 hours.

• Adjust oven rack to lowest position and preheat oven to 400°F.
• Pat rabbit pieces dry.
• Dice bacon, shallots and peeled carrots.
• Heat oil and butter in flameproof casserole. Add bacon and cook over medium heat, stirring frequently, until fat is rendered. Remove with slotted spoon and set aside.
• Add rabbit pieces to casserole in batches and brown well on all sides, removing each batch as it is cooked.
• Add shallots and carrots and cook, stirring, until almost tender. Return rabbit pieces to casserole with bacon and remaining wine. Scrape up browned bits from bottom of casserole.
• Season mixture with salt and white pepper. Add thyme, bay leaf and whole spices. Cover and bake 40 minutes.
• Stir stew twice during cooking, braising rabbit with pan liquid.
• Add prunes with marinating liquid and mix carefully. Pour in cream. Bake another 30 minutes. Serve piping hot with *spaetzle* or French or Italian bread.

Venison Goulash, Russian Style

Allow plenty of time for this dish, because it must marinate awhile.

The best cut is shoulder of venison; ask the butcher to trim it of all fat, membrane and gristle. Don't buy the canned venison "ragout" or "goulash" that sometimes appears in fancy food shops; it is usually made from different parts of the animal that cook at different rates.

1 onion
2 bunches soup greens
2 pounds boneless venison, cut into cubes
1 whole clove
1 bay leaf
2 cups dry red wine
1½ ounces (40 grams) dried mushrooms
¼ cup vegetable oil
1 tablespoon all-purpose flour
2 tablespoons raspberry vinegar
Salt and freshly ground black pepper
1 fresh beet
2 dill pickles
1 cup crème fraîche or sour cream

4 servings
500 calories per serving
Preparation time: about 1¾ hours
Marinating time: 6 hours

Finely chop onion. Trim and wash soup greens; chop finely.

• Combine meat, onion, soup greens, clove and bay leaf in mixing bowl. Pour in wine and marinate in a cool place for 6 hours.

• Cover dried mushrooms with lukewarm water and let soak 4 hours.

• Remove meat from marinade and pat dry. Strain marinade.

• Heat oil in large deep skillet. Add meat and brown over high high heat. Add onion and soup greens and sauté briefly.

• Sprinkle mixture with flour and cook until flour is browned. Pour in vinegar and strained marinade. Season with salt and pepper. Cover and cook over low heat 45 minutes.

• Meanwhile, peel and wash beet. Slice, then cut slices into sticks. Add to meat and cook 15 minutes. Add mushrooms with soaking water (strain if necessary) and cook 15 minutes longer.

• Cut pickles into sticks and stir into goulash with crème fraîche. Heat through, but do not cook further. Serve.

Ratatouille

A colorful vegetable stew, Provençal style.

1 generous pound small, slender eggplants
Salt
1 generous pound small zucchini
1 generous pound mixed green, red and yellow bell peppers
1 generous pound tomatoes
1 onion
3 garlic cloves
½ cold-pressed olive oil
Freshly ground black pepper
2 sprigs thyme
1 sprig rosemary
¼ bunch parsley
1 bay leaf
Additional olive oil for sprinkling

6 servings
400 calories per serving
Preparation time: about 1¼ hours

Wash eggplants and blot dry. Cut into ¼-inch crosswise slices, discarding stem and blossom ends.
• Sprinkle slices with salt on both sides (the salt will draw out some of the eggplant's moisture, so it will not spatter as much on frying and it will absorb less oil).

• Let eggplant stand 10 minutes, then carefully pat dry with paper towels.
• Wash and dry zucchini; cut into ¼-inch slices, discarding ends. Quarter peppers; discard stems, seeds and membranes. Rinse peppers in cold water and pat thoroughly dry. Cut each quarter into two or three lengthwise slices. Pour boiling water over tomatoes and let stand briefly, then plunge tomatoes into ice water. Peel tomatoes and halve or quarter lengthwise. Discard stems and seeds. Cut onion into very thin, even slices.
• Using a small, sharp knife, cut garlic into strips, then into very fine dice.

• Adjust oven rack to second position from bottom and preheat oven to 425°F.
• Heat some of olive oil in large skillet. Add eggplant slices and sauté on both sides until browned but not soft. Remove from skillet and drain on paper towels.

• Fry remaining vegetables separately in batches, adding oil to skillet as necessary. Transfer each vegetable to separate plate as it is cooked.
• Layer vegetables in shallow ovenproof casserole, seasoning each layer with salt and pepper.
• Rinse thyme, rosemary and parsley under cold running water. Shake dry or, better, pat dry with paper towels.

• Tie fresh herbs and bay leaf into a bundle with kitchen string (this will make herbs easy to retrieve after cooking and keep any hard stems from being left behind).
• Lay herb bundle on top of vegetables and sprinkle ratatouille with olive oil (close off half the bottle opening with your thumb for easiesr sprinkling).
• Bake ratatouille 30 minutes. Remove from oven; if there is a lot of accumulated liquid, pour it off into a saucepan and boil

down to desired consistency, then return to vegetables.
• Serve ratatouille hot or let cool to lukewarm. Fresh French bread or dark rye bread and butter makes a good partner.

Variation: Peperonata

Quarter lengthwise 2¼ pounds mixed red, green and yellow bell peppers. Remove stems, seeds and membranes. Rinse peppers under cold water and pat dry. Peel 1 generous pound ripe tomatoes; discard stems and seeds. Coarsely chop tomatoes. Coarsely chop 2 large onions; halve 3 garlic cloves. Heat 2 tablespoons olive oil in large saucepan. Add onion and garlic and cook until translucent. Add vegetables and pour 6 to 7 tablespoons olive oil over. Add 2 sprigs each thyme, rosemary and oregano. Cover and cook over low heat 30 minutes, stirring frequently. Season with salt and freshly ground black pepper.

This specialty of Nice is at its best during the summer, since it really should be made only with fresh, sun-ripened vegetables and fragrant fresh herbs. The original recipe called for a cooking time of at least 1 hour, but this results in vegetables that are soggy and overcooked. We follow the more modern trend, cooking the ratatouille only half as long; it is tender and juicy, but still has some "tooth." Ratatouille can be served warm or cold. It is good both as a first course and as a main dish (for four people), and will keep well in the refrigerator for three days.

Pizza Succulenta

Ideal for parties.

1¾ cups all-purpose flour

1 cake fresh or 1 envelope active dry yeast

½ cup lukewarm water

Salt

2 large cans (28 ounces each) peeled tomatoes

2 garlic cloves

Olive oil

Freshly ground black pepper

1 teaspoon crushed dried oregano

1 bunch basil

Flour for rolling dough

2 tablespoons anchovy paste

5 ounces fresh mushrooms

5 ounces lean cooked ham

2 ounces black olives

8 mild green pickled chili peppers

5 bottled artichoke hearts

4 anchovy fillets

14 ounces (about) mozzarella cheese

2 tablespoons freshly grated pecorino or Parmesan cheese

4 servings
825 calories per serving
Preparation time: about 1 hour
Resting time: about 45 minutes

Sift flour into mixing bowl. Make a well in center and sprinkle in yeast.

• Pour part of the lukewarm water over yeast and stir briskly to incorporate yeast and some of the flour from the edge of the well into a sponge. Cover with towel and let rest 10 to 15 minutes.

• Add remaining water and a generous pinch of salt and blend to form smooth, elastic dough. Beat until bubbles form and dough comes away from side of bowl. Cover with towel and let rest 30 minutes.

• Meanwhile, drain tomatoes in colander or sieve. Chop finely. Mince or press garlic.

• Heat about 3 tablespoons olive oil in large saucepan, add garlic and cook very briefly; do not brown. Add tomatoes, season with salt, pepper and oregano and simmer until thickened. Let cool slightly.

• Rinse basil and shake dry. Cut leaves into fine julienne.

• Turn dough out onto floured surface and knead until elastic and no longer sticky.

• Oil two pizza pans or a large baking sheet.

• Halve dough; roll out each half into a thin circle. Transfer to prepared pan(s).

• Blend anchovy paste with about 2 tablespoons olive oil and spread evenly over dough. Prick dough with fork so that it will rise evenly and will not form large bubbles.

• Stir basil into cooled tomato sauce and spread over pizzas.

• Clean and slice mushrooms. Cut ham into strips.

• Adjust rack to center of oven and preheat oven to 400°F.

• Drain olives, peppers, artichoke hearts and anchovies. Halve olives, quarter artichoke hearts and cut anchovies into small pieces. Cut mozzarella into small slices.

• Divide all these ingredients over pizzas.

• Sprinkle evenly with grated cheese and drizzle generously with olive oil.

• Bake pizzas 15 to 20 minutes, or until crust is cooked through and edges are crisp.

Tip: You may, of course, roll out dough into a large rectangle and bake one pizza rather than two.

Variation: Pizza Margherita

This easily prepared pizza displays the colors of the Italian flag. Spread dough with peeled, seeded tomato slices or pureed tomatoes. Top with mozzarella slices and basil leaves. Season with salt and drizzle with olive oil.

Variation: Pizza alla Marinara

The topping here consists of peeled, seeded and well-drained tomato pieces, garlic slices, anchovy fillets and lots of olive oil. Sprinkle a few capers here and there and season very generously with freshly ground black pepper.

Variation: Pizza Quattro Stagioni

This "four seasons" pizza is among the most popular of all in its homeland. Lightly score dough circle into quarters with the back of a knife, or divide into quarters with two thin crosswise strips of dough. Each quarter gets a different topping—for example, mussels in the first, anchovies, olives and garlic in the second, tomatoes, mozzarella and basil in the third and quartered artichoke hearts and ham strips in the fourth. Drizzle whole pizza generously with olive oil and sprinkle with crushed dried oregano if you wish.

Originally, pizza was a simple flatbread topped only with garlic, herbs, olives or pork cracklings. Much later the first tomato-topped pizza was developed in Naples—and the Neopolitans are very proud of their beloved *pizza napoletana*. For that version the dough is topped with peeled, seeded and well-blotted tomato slices, which in turn are sprinkled with crushed oregano (sometimes a few basil leaves also) and sliced garlic. The whole is drizzled liberally with olive oil. Our more elaborate recipe is one example of a particularly flavorful variation.

Lasagne Verdi al Forno (Baked Spinach Lasagne)

This takes some time to assemble, but it's more than worth it.

8 ounces green lasagne noodles
Salt
3 ounces bacon
2 onions
3 garlic cloves
3 celery stalks
2 carrots
3 tomatoes
¼ cup olive oil
10 to 11 ounces mixed ground meat or meat loaf mixture
½ cup hot meat broth
⅓ to ½ cup dry red wine
1 tablespoon tomato paste
Freshly ground black pepper
Pinch of sugar
4 sprigs oregano
½ bunch parsley
6 tablespoons heavy cream
¼ cup (½ stick) butter
½ cup all-purpose flour
3 cups hot milk
Freshly ground white pepper
Freshly grated nutmeg
7 ounces mozzarella cheese
Butter for baking dish
3 ounces (about ¾ cup) freshly grated Parmesan cheese

6 servings
830 calories per serving
Preparation time: about 2 hours

Check lasagne package to see whether noodles must be cooked before assembling dish; there are some types appearing on the market that do not require precooking. If noodles must be cooked, bring large pot of salted water to boil, add noodles and cook according to package directions.
• Drain noodles and drop into cold water; drain thoroughly, preferably on rack.
• Dice bacon very finely. Finely chop onions; mince or press garlic.

• Using a paring knife, lift up coarse strings from bottom ends of celery stalks and strip strings away. Cut stalks lengthwise into fine strips, then crosswise into tiny cubes. Finely chop leaves.
• Peel and finely dice carrots. Pour boiling water over tomatoes; peel, stem, seed and finely chop.
• Cook bacon in large saucepan until fat is rendered. Add olive oil and heat thoroughly, then add all prepared vegetables except tomatoes and cook, stirring, until liquid has evaporated.
• Stir in ground meat and cook until crumbly and browned. Add tomatoes and hot broth.

• Pour in wine, stir in tomato paste and season with salt, pepper and sugar.
• Rinse herbs and shake dry; chop finely. Stir into saucepan. Cover and cook 20 minutes over gentle heat, stirring occasionally. Blend in cream.
• While this Bolognese sauce is cooking, prepare béchamel sauce. Melt butter in another saucepan, whisk in flour and cook gently.

• As soon as surface of mixture is covered with a whitish foam, whisk in hot milk. Cook sauce over low heat 10 minutes, until thick and creamy. Season with salt, white pepper and nutmeg.

• Slice mozzarella; cut slices into small cubes. Butter a 13 × 9-inch baking dish. Adjust rack to center of oven and preheat oven to 400°F.

• Line baking dish with a layer of lasagne noodles (if using uncooked noodles, first spread a thin layer of béchamel sauce in dish). Spread evenly with Bolognese sauce.
• Spoon some of béchamel over meat sauce; sprinkle with some mozzarella and Parmesan. Cover with more lasagne noodles and repeat layers until all ingredients are used.

• The last layer should consist of béchamel and cheese.
• Bake 25 to 30 minutes, or until top is golden brown. If lasagne is to be served as a main dish, accompany with a green or mixed salad; the salad can be omitted if lasagne is served as an appetizer or pasta course (in which case it will serve 10).

This baked green noodle specialty is very popular in its Italian homeland, where it is sometimes a first course, sometimes a snack, and less frequently a main dish. The ingredients can vary somewhat, as Italian cooks often add leftovers—perhaps a few cut-up artichoke hearts, some peas, olives, or mushrooms, a bit of spinach. Other common additions are chicken, chicken livers, anchovy fillets and bits of ham. Of course, plain lasagne noodles can be used in place of spinach noodles.

Spaghetti *al Pesto*

In Italy this is usually a first course; we are more accustomed to having it with a salad as entree.

People tend to think that anyone can cook spaghetti—and consequently they make a lot of mistakes. Buy only the best-quality pasta; it is always worth the difference in price. Cook it in a large amount of rapidly boiling water, using a generous quart of water and about 2 teaspoons salt for each 4 ounces of pasta.

| 4 to 5 garlic cloves |
| ⅓ cup pine nuts |
| 3 bunches basil |
| Salt and freshly ground white pepper |
| ½ cup cold-pressed olive oil |
| 2 to 3 tablespoons freshly grated pecorino cheese |
| 4 generous quarts water |
| Dash of olive oil |
| 1 pound spaghetti |

4 servings
790 calories per serving
Preparation time: about 1 hour

Finely chop garlic and pine nuts.

• Rinse basil and pat dry; cut leaves into strips. Crush in a mortar with 2 to 3 pinches of salt (or grind basil in blender or processor).
• Add garlic and pine nuts to basil, season with white pepper and blend to a smooth paste, gradually adding olive oil and pecorino. Cover pesto and set aside.
• Combine water and 2 rounded tablespoons salt in a large pot and bring to

boil; maintain at a full boil for at least 2 to 3 minutes.
• Add a generous dash of olive oil to help keep pasta from sticking together during cooking. When water returns to rapid boil, gradually add spaghetti. Cook, stirring frequently, until al dente (cooking time will depend on freshness and thickness of spaghetti). To test pasta for doneness, remove a strand as soon as its yellowish color has paled somewhat; the center should not be hard, but it should retain some firmness. Drain spaghetti in colander, reserving 2 to 3 tablespoons

cooking water; do not rinse. Shake pasta as dry as possible, then transfer to heated serving bowl.
• Mix reserved cooking water into pesto; spoon over pasta.

Variation: Spaghetti with Tomato Sauce (pictured upper left)

Peel and finely chop 1 pound, 10 ounces tomatoes and 3 to 4 garlic cloves. Heat 6 to 8 tablespoons olive oil, add garlic and cook until translucent. Stir in tomatoes and season with salt, black pepper, a pinch of sugar and a generous ½ teaspoon oregano. Cover halfway and cook until thickened to desired sauce consistency. Meanwhile, cook 1 pound spaghetti. Finely chop 1 bunch basil. Mix into sauce, then spoon over well-drained pasta.

Tip: The third sauce in the photograph (upper right) is Bolognese sauce, prepared as in the recipe for *Lasagne Verdi al Forno* on page 72/73 and enriched with ½ ounce (15 grams) dried porcini mushrooms, soaked and finely chopped.

Spaghetti Carbonara

This is perfect for unexpected guests. Made with ingredients that are usually on hand, it can be whipped up at a moment's notice and it tastes wonderful. Pecorino, the Italian sheep's-milk cheese, can be substituted for Parmesan.

A rich, satisfying dish.

2 tablespoons cold-pressed olive oil
Salt
8 to 9 ounces lean bacon
Freshly ground black pepper
1 pound spaghetti
6 egg yolks
½ cup heavy cream
3 to 4 ounces (about ¾ to 1 cup) freshly grated Parmesan cheese
1 ounce (about ¼ cup) freshly grated pecorino cheese

4 servings
980 calories per serving
Preparation time: about 30 minutes

In a large pot combine 4 quarts water, 1 tablespoon olive oil and about 3 tablespoons salt; bring to boil.
• Meanwhile, dice bacon, trimming away any tough rind.
• Heat remaining olive oil. Add bacon and cook over medium heat, stirring, until fat is rendered and meat is crisp. Season generously with pepper during cooking.

• Remove bacon with slotted spoon or skimmer and drain on several layers of paper towel. Invert a bowl over bacon to keep warm.
• Cook spaghetti in rapidly boiling water, stirring frequently, until al dente.
• Meanwhile, blend egg yolks with cream and both cheeses. Warm over low heat, stirring constantly, until cheese is completely melted. Stir in 2 tablespoons spaghetti cooking water.
• Drain spaghetti in colander and shake as dry as possible. Transfer to heated bowl and toss with yolk mixture and bacon bits. Season with salt and freshly ground pepper. Serve with additional grated cheese and a tossed salad.

Saltimbocca alla Romana

Fresh sage provides the special flavor here.

Italian cuisine includes many meat specialties, but because meat is expensive there they are prepared with great care and generally served in small portions. A prime example is this exquisite dish, whose name appropriately means "jump in the mouth."

8 small veal scallops, about 3 ounces each
Freshly ground white pepper
16 fresh sage leaves
8 thin slices prosciutto
1 tablespoon (about) all-purpose flour
¼ cup (½ stick) butter
½ cup dry white wine
Salt

4 servings
410 calories per serving
Preparation time: about 30 minutes

Lightly flatten veal scallops by patting with fingertips until meat is spread out to twice its original dimensions; do not use meat mallet. Pat dry on both sides with paper towels. Season with white pepper and press in firmly.

• Rinse sage leaves briefly under cold water and carefully pat dry. Lay 2 leaves on each veal scallop and cover with a slice of prosciutto.

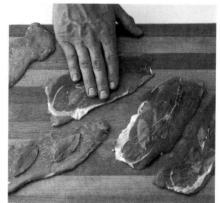

• Press prosciutto firmly against veal, spreading it to edges of veal and smoothing out any ripples or bubbles, which will keep ham from binding well to veal. Turn each piece over so that prosciutto side is down.

• Place flour in small strainer and sift a very thin layer over meat. Press into meat with hands, paying special attention to edges so that veal and ham are sealed together.

• Heat a large, heavy skillet and add ⅔ of the butter; heat until butter begins to foam but is not browned.

• Add as many pieces of meat, prosciutto side down, as will fit comfortably in skillet (it is important that the prosciutto side cook first, or ham and veal will not hold together and will have to be secured with skewers or toothpicks).

• Cook scallops 2 to 3 minutes on each side; transfer to heated platter and keep warm.

• Pour wine into skillet and deglaze over high heat, scraping up browned bits and boiling until sauce is reduced and creamy. Season with salt and white pepper. Remove from heat and whisk in remaining butter, cut into small bits.

• Season *saltimbocca* on both sides with pepper and just a little salt (prosciutto is already salted). Pour sauce around (not over) meat and serve at once. Accompany with a salad or buttered vegetables and Italian bread, risotto or—not traditional, but delicious—*rösti* potatoes.

Scaloppine al Limone

1/2 recipe

Scaloppine are very small, thin veal cutlets; Italian cooks prepare them in countless ways. This variation is particularly good with fresh lime, but you can certainly use lemon if you prefer.

A quick and fresh-tasting Italian summertime dish.

8 small veal scallops, about 2½ ounces each
Salt and freshly ground white pepper
1½ tablespoons (about) all-purpose flour
3 tablespoons butter
2 limes (or lemons)
1 scant cup Italian dry white wine
½ bunch parsley, chopped (optional)

4 servings
320 calories per serving
Preparation time: about 20 minutes

Pat veal scallops dry with paper towels and flatten as much as possible with fingertips.

• Season with salt and pepper on both sides and flour meat lightly, pressing flour in well (this will protect the tender meat fibers from drying out).
• Melt butter in skillet over moderate heat; do not brown. Add veal and cook about 1 minute per side. Transfer to heated platter and keep warm. *4*
• Wash and dry limes; cut *8* thin slices. Squeeze juice from remaining fruit.
• Pour wine into skillet and deglaze over high heat, scraping up browned bits and boiling until sauce is slightly thickened. Season with lime juice, salt and white pepper; add parsley if desired. Pour sauce around (not over) veal.
• Place lime slice on each scallop and serve immediately with buttered vegetables, a salad and boiled potatoes, or Italian bread.

Risotto with Spinach and Pine Nuts

The rice here is both creamy and chewy.

1 onion
1 garlic clove
7 ounces sliced boiled ham
10 to 11 ounces fresh spinach
2 tablespoons cold-pressed olive oil
1¾ cups Italian arborio rice
4 to 5 cups meat broth
½ cup Italian dry white wine
Salt and freshly ground white pepper
3 tablespoons butter
2 tablespoons pine nuts
3 ounces (about ¾ cup) freshly grated Parmesan cheese

4 servings
795 calories per serving
Preparation time: about 50 minutes

Finely chop onion. Chop garlic; finely dice ham.
- Sort spinach, trimming away tough stems. Wash leaves well and shake dry.

- Using a large knife, cut spinach into strips, then chop coarsely.
- Heat olive oil in large saucepan. Add onion and garlic and sauté over medium heat until translucent, stirring frequently. Add ham and cook 1 minute.

- Sprinkle in rice and cook, stirring, 2 minutes to coat thoroughly with oil. (Do not wash rice first; washing will remove the starch coating that makes rice cohesive, as it should be for risotto.)

- Pour in half of broth and bring to boil over high heat. Reduce heat to low; from this point on, if heat is too high the liquid will evaporate too quickly and rice will not become tender.
- Stir in chopped spinach.

- Pour in wine and season with salt and white pepper. Continue cooking until rice is tender, about 30 minutes, gradually adding broth as it is absorbed and stirring very frequently with fork or wooden spoon to keep rice from sticking.
- While rice cooks, melt ½ tablespoon butter in very small saucepan.
- Add pine nuts to butter and cook, stirring, over low heat until golden brown. Add to risotto with remaining butter and grated Parmesan and stir with fork to blend well. Transfer to heated bowl and serve immediately.

Variation: Lamb Pilaf

Soak 10 dried apricots in water to cover overnight. Rinse, dry and dice 1 medium eggplant. Sprinkle with salt and let stand 10 minutes to drain, then pat eggplant dry with paper towels. Cut about 1 pound boneless leg of lamb into ¾-inch cubes. Finely chop 1 large onion and 2 garlic cloves. Heat 2 tablespoons vegetable oil in large flameproof casserole. Add lamb in batches and brown over high heat; remove meat as it is cooked and drain in sieve or colander set over a plate. Sauté eggplant cubes in 2 additional tablespoons oil; remove and set aside. Add more oil to pan if necessary and sauté onion and garlic until translucent. Return meat to saucepan and pour in ½ cup meat broth. Season with salt and freshly ground black pepper. Cover and braise on bottom rack of preheated 350°F oven for 30 minutes. Meanwhile, remove stem, seeds and membranes from 1 red bell pepper; cut pepper into fine strips. Chop 1 piece crystallized ginger. Drain apricots and chop coarsely. Toast a scant ½ cup pine nuts in heavy ungreased skillet. Add red pepper, ginger, apricots, pine nuts and eggplant to lamb mixture and stir through; cover and return to oven for 25 minutes. Rinse ⅔ cup long-grain rice and sauté in 1 tablespoon oil until translucent. Pour in 1¾ cups cold water. Bring to boil, then cook over low heat until tender but not mushy, about 20 minutes. Mix cooked rice into lamb and flavor with the juice of ½ lemon.

The best risotto is made with imported arborio rice, which can be purchased at Italian markets and gourmet specialty shops. Starchier than the long-grain type, arborio rice holds together when cooked; it should come out thick and viscous, not dry and fluffy, and the individual rice grains should be firm to the tooth. Risotto can be served as a main course or side dish, depending on its ingredients. When flavored just with Parmesan and butter it makes an excellent accompaniment to quick-sautéed meats, while this spinach risotto constitutes a complete meal.

Sweet and Sour Pork

This must be cooked at the last minute and served right away.

1¼ pounds boneless pork butt or fresh ham

1 egg

6 tablespoons cornstarch

2 scant tablespoons all-purpose flour

Freshly ground white pepper

¼ cup soy sauce

3 tablespoons rice wine or dry Sherry

1 cup cold meat broth

1 small red bell pepper

2 carrots

1 small cucumber (3 to 4 ounces)

2 celery stalks with leaves

1 garlic clove

Peanut or vegetable oil for deep frying

1 tablespoon peanut oil

Salt

3 tablespoons ketchup

⅓ cup red wine vinegar

Juice of 1 orange

1½ teaspoons fresh lemon juice

⅓ cup sugar

2 tablespooons cold water

Sambal oelek

4 servings
650 calories per serving
Preparation time: about 45 minutes
Resting time: about 30 minutes

Trim all fat from pork; cut meat into ¾-inch cubes.
• Separate egg; refrigerate white. Set aside 1 heaping tablespoon cornstarch.

• Whisk egg yolk with remaining cornstarch, flour and pepper. Blend in 1 tablespoon each soy sauce and rice wine or Sherry. Add enough meat broth to make a smooth batter that is thick enough to coat meat cubes. Cover and let stand 30 minutes.
• Combine 2 tablespoons each soy sauce and rice wine. Add meat cubes, cover and marinate 10 minutes, stirring several times.
• Meanwhile, halve bell pepper and remove stem, seeds and membranes. Rinse pepper halves under cold water and pat dry; cut into strips. Peel and wash carrots and cut into thin sticks. Peel cucumber and cut into strips. Wash and dry celery; remove tough outer strings. Chop leaves coarsely and set aside. Cut stalks into finger-thick slices. Mince garlic.
• Preheat oven to 275°F. Line baking sheet with paper towels and place in oven.
• Beat egg white until stiff and fold into prepared batter.

• Heat oil for deep frying until a cube of white bread dropped into oil browns quickly.
• Coat meat cubes with batter in batches and fry until golden brown. Remove with slotted spoon, arrange in single layer on paper towel-lined baking sheet and keep warm.
• Heat peanut oil in skillet. Add garlic and cook over medium heat until translucent. Season with salt. Add remaining soy sauce, ketchup, vinegar, orange and lemon juices and sugar and cook, stirring, until sugar is dissolved.

• Pour in remaining meat broth and bring to boil. Add vegetables and cook over medium-low heat until crisp-tender, about 6 to 8 minutes.

• Mix remaining cornstarch with water and stir into vegetables. Bring to boil and season with *sambal oelek*. Stir in meat cubes and sprinkle with celery leaves. Serve immediately with steamed rice.

Variation:
Chinese Vegetables

Cover ¾ ounce (25 grams) dried Oriental mushrooms with water and soak 3 hours. Trim away hard stems; coarsely chop caps. Peel and chop a ¾-inch piece of fresh ginger root and 1 garlic clove. Peel and trim 2 carrots and cut into sticks; slice 2 celery stalks; trim 1 bunch scallions and cut into ½-inch lengths. Thinly slice 4 ounces bamboo shoot. Rinse and drain 4 ounces fresh soybean sprouts. Mix ½ cup chicken broth, 1 tablespoon dry Sherry and 2 tablespoons soy sauce. Heat 2 tablespoons peanut oil in large skillet or wok. Add about ½ teaspoon salt, ginger and garlic and stir-fry briefly over high heat. Add carrots and stir-fry 2 minutes. Add remaining vegetables and mushrooms and cook another 2 minutes. Pour in broth mixture and bring quickly to boil, then reduce heat to low, cover and simmer 3 to 4 minutes. Serve hot.

As is the case with most Chinese dishes, this sweet and sour pork is made in an exact progression of closely-timed cooking steps. Have all ingredients prepared before you begin cooking. The meat should be cooked in small batches to ensure crispness; after frying it is kept warm in a low oven. (Be sure the pieces do not touch each other, or the crust will soften.) For authentic flavor and texture the sauce must also be prepared quickly, so that the vegetables remain crisp.

Classic Omelet

A perfect omelet is smooth and even outside, soft and moist within. Success depends above all on the cook's instinct and experience; if you need practice, divide the ingredients by four and make a few omelets just for yourself.

This demands quick and careful timing.

8 large, fresh eggs
Salt and freshly ground white pepper
¼ cup (½ stick) butter

4 servings
300 calories per serving
Preparation time: about 10 minutes per omelet

Break 2 eggs into shallow bowl or deep plate. (Do not use a deep bowl, as it will not permit you to mix the eggs quickly enough.) Season with salt and pepper.
• Place an ungreased heavy 8-inch skillet over high heat until very hot. Reduce heat to medium-low and melt a piece of butter in skillet without browning.
• While butter melts, quickly beat eggs with fork just until white and yolk are blended. Do not use whisk or beater; this will introduce air into eggs and the resulting omelet will be tough. It is also important to mix and cook only a single-serving omelet at a time, because eggs should be cooked immediately after mixing.

• Tip and rotate skillet in all directions to coat evenly with butter. As soon as butter starts to foam, pour in eggs and stir very quickly with back of fork to bring most of egg in contact with skillet.
• As soon as egg begins to set, run fork around edge of omelet and loosen from one side of skillet. Hold skillet at a slant so that uncooked egg can flow to bottom of pan and set. Tap skillet handle with your fingertips; edges of omelet should come away slightly from pan.

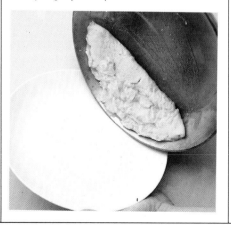

• Using fork, lightly roll and push omelet to middle of pan. Tilt skillet so that omelet lies to one side in half-moon shape. Gently lift unrolled edge of omelet with fork; bring over rest of omelet and press lightly.
• Tilt pan to front and let omelet slide out onto heated plate. If desired, pat into shape and keep warm with napkin.
• Prepare remaining omelets in the same manner.

Variation: Herb Omelet

For each serving add 1 to 2 tablespoons chopped fresh herbs to blended eggs. Chervil, parsley and sorrel are particularly good.

Savory Stuffed Crepes

A piquant filling turns simple crepes into a real treat. Feel free to incorporate leftovers into the filling if you like. It saves time to cook the crepes ahead, stack them between sheets of foil or waxed paper, and freeze them.

Thrifty and easily prepared ahead of time.

1 cup plus 2 tablespoons all-purpose flour
Salt
1½ cups milk
2 eggs
7 tablespoons butter, melted
1 onion
10 to 11 ounces boiled ham, finely diced
1 cup heavy cream
½ bunch chervil, chopped
½ bunch parsley, chopped
Grated peel of ½ lemon
4 ounces Emmental cheese, grated
Freshly ground white pepper

4 servings
900 calories per serving
Preparation time: about 1 hour

Combine flour and salt. Gradually whisk in 1 cup milk and eggs. Let batter rest 30 minutes.
• Reserve 1 tablespoon melted butter.

• Heat remaining butter a small amount at a time in 8-inch skillet. Ladle in a portion of batter, rotating skillet to cover bottom evenly. Cook crepe until bottom is browned and top is firm. Turn and cook second side. Repeat process to make 9 to 10 thin crepes.
• Adjust oven rack to second position from bottom and preheat oven to 400°F.
• Chop onion. Heat remaining melted butter, add onion and cook until translucent. Add ham and sauté. Pour in half of cream and cook over high heat, stirring, until thick.
• Blend in herbs, lemon peel and cheese; season filling with salt and white pepper.
• Spread one side of each crepe with filling; roll up and arrange side by side in baking dish.
• Blend remaining cream and remaining milk and pour over crepes. Bake until golden brown, about 20 minutes. Serve piping hot.

Stuffed Peppers

Refreshingly simple to prepare.

1 large onion
3 garlic cloves
¼ cup olive oil
⅓ cup long-grain rice
14 ounces mixed ground meat (not too lean)
½ cup meat broth
2¾ pounds ripe tomatoes
Salt and freshly ground black pepper
1 bunch chives
¼ bunch parsley, chopped
1 tablespoon drained capers
4 equal-size bell peppers
1 small can (6 ounces) tomato paste
Pinch of sugar
Meat broth or dry red wine, if needed
½ bunch basil, chopped

4 servings
520 calories per serving
Preparation time: about 1¼ hours

Finely chop onion and garlic. Reserve half of each for tomato sauce.
• Heat 3 tablespoons olive oil in large saucepan. Add rice and stir over high heat until translucent. Add onion and garlic and sauté until they are also translucent.

• Add meat and cook, stirring, until crumbly and browned.
• Pour in meat broth and scrape up browned bits from bottom of pan. Bring to boil, then cover and simmer over low heat until rice is nearly cooked, about 10 minutes (rice must still be firm or it will be too soft by the time peppers are cooked).
• Pour boiling water over tomatoes, let stand briefly and then plunge into cold water. Peel and halve tomatoes.

• Holding each tomato half in one hand, squeeze out seeds with light pressure; trim away stem. Thinly slice 2 tomato halves for filling; dice remaining tomatoes.
• Season meat mixture with salt and plenty of pepper.
• Rinse chives and pat dry. Snip into tiny rings.
• Mix chives, parsley, capers and thinly sliced tomato into meat.

• Starting about ⅜ inch below stem end, cut horizontally across each pepper to form a lid. Remove seeds and membranes. Rinse peppers and tops and pat dry.
• Stuff peppers with meat mixture and top with pepper "lids." Set aside.
• For tomato sauce, heat 1 tablespoon olive oil in large saucepan. Add remaining onion and garlic and sauté until translucent. Stir in diced tomatoes and tomato paste. Season with salt, freshly ground pepper and sugar. Cover and simmer over low heat 10 minutes, adding a bit of broth or wine if sauce is too thick (if necessary, season again with salt and pepper).

• Place stuffed peppers in sauce, cover and cook over low heat about 40 minutes.
• Remove peppers from sauce and keep warm. Purée or strain sauce and reheat. Stir in basil. Serve peppers in sauce; accompany with boiled potatoes or rice.

Variation: Eggplant-Stuffed Peppers

Wash and dry 1 eggplant (do not peel); cut into ⅜-inch cubes. Sprinkle with salt and let stand 10 minutes to drain. Transfer eggplant to kitchen towel and pat dry. Heat 6 tablespoons olive oil in large skillet. Add eggplant and sauté on all sides; remove with slotted spoon. Add 5 ounces diced prosciutto and 2 chopped garlic cloves to skillet and sauté. Add 2 medium-size peeled and seeded tomatoes and cook briefly. Combine tomato mixture with 10 to 11 ounces finely diced mozzarella and egg-plant cubes. Season with salt, freshly ground black pepper and 1 tablespoon chopped fresh thyme. Divide among 4 prepared pepper shells. Cook tomato sauce as above, add stuffed peppers and cook over low heat about 40 minutes—or instead of tomato sauce use about 1 cup hot meat broth for cooking peppers. In the latter case, remove peppers at end of cooking time and whisk some heavy cream or crème fraîche into cooking liquid; boil over high heat until reduced to desired sauce consistency.

Bell peppers are abundant and fresh in the markets during the summer. A truly fresh pepper has firm flesh and taut, smooth skin, without any bruises or soft spots. For stuffing, look for large, well-rounded peppers with thick walls; long, slender peppers are better reserved for salads. Don't use very lean meat, or the stuffing is likely to be dry; you can add moisture with juicy ingredients such as tomatoes, bacon, and soaked, squeezed bread cubes. Flavor the filling with plenty of aromatic herbs—chives, basil, parsley or thyme.

Green Beans with Bacon

A tasty side dish, quickly put together.

| 5 ounces bacon |
| 1 onion |
| 2 garlic cloves |
| Salt |
| 1 generous pound tomatoes |
| 1 pound, 10 ounces green beans |
| ½ bunch summer savory |
| 1 tablespoon cold-pressed olive oil |
| ½ cup meat broth |
| ¼ cup dry red wine |
| Freshly ground black pepper |
| Pinch of sugar |
| ½ bunch basil |
| 1 tablespoon tomato paste |

4 servings
450 calories per person
Preparation time: about 40 minutes

Finely dice bacon, discarding any rind. Finely chop onion.

• Coarsely chop garlic. Sprinkle with salt and crush finely with a large, heavy knife blade. (The salt will help keep garlic from sliding out from beneath blade.)
• Pour boiling water over tomatoes, let stand briefly and plunge into cold water. Peel tomatoes, halve horizontally and squeeze out seeds. Trim away stems and dice flesh.
• Bring a large pot of salted water to rapid boil to blanch beans.
• Meanwhile, wash beans in cold water; drain. Trim ends; remove strings if necessary (but it rarely is with the bean varieties grown nowadays).
• Drop whole beans into boiling water and blanch over high heat 4 minutes, then remove with skimmer and drop into ice water to stop cooking process.

(Blanching and quick chilling help preserve beans' bright green color during subsequent cooking.) Drain well.
• Rinse savory and shake dry. Set aside some leaves for garnish.

• Heat olive oil in large skillet. Add diced bacon and cook over medium-low heat, stirring frequently, until meat is crisp and fat foams lightly. Do not cook over higher heat or bacon will burn before sufficient fat is rendered.
• Add onion to skillet and cook over medium heat until translucent, stirring frequently. Adjust heat as necessary, for onions also burn easily and will taste bitter if they do.
• When onion is translucent, reduce heat, add garlic to skillet and cook, stirring, until it is limp and translucent and onion is lightly colored. (Garlic should always be cooked briefly and over gentle heat.)

• Add tomatoes to skillet and stir through. Cover and cook 2 minutes to release juices. Increase heat.

• Stir in blanched beans, broth and wine and bring to boil.
• Season mixture with pepper and sugar; salt lightly (bacon is already salty). Taste and adjust seasoning. Lay savory sprigs on vegetables, cover and cook over low heat about 15 minutes, or until beans are tender but not too soft.
• Meanwhile, wash basil and shake dry. Set aside a few leaves for garnish; coarsely chop remainder.
• Discard savory from vegetables. Stir in tomato paste and chopped basil.
• Transfer beans to heated serving bowl and sprinkle with reserved savory and basil leaves. Beans are especially good served with pork chops or steak and French or Italian bread.

Variation:
Haricots Verts à la Française

Substitute 1 pound, 10 ounces *haricots verts* for regular green beans; blanch in boiling salted water 3 minutes. Plunge beans into ice water and drain. Melt 5 tablespoons butter in large saucepan over medium heat; do not brown. Stir in juice of ½ lemon and ½ bunch finely chopped parsley. Add beans, cover and cook over low heat 10 minutes, or until tender but still firm. Season with salt and freshly ground white pepper.

The first fresh green beans start coming to the markets in May, and the various types can be recognized by their shapes: Flat, wide runner beans, up to 8 inches or so in length, are thick-fleshed and must be "snapped" into shorter lengths before cooking. Bush beans, with round to oval pods, can be used whole or broken into smaller pieces; they are good for side dishes and salads. *Haricots verts*, the finest green beans of all, have slim, tender pods that are cooked whole. Finally, there are yellow wax beans, most commonly used in salads.

Stuffed Zucchini

A new version of an old favorite.

4 zucchini, about 7 ounces each
10 to 11 ounces chicken livers
1 onion
1 garlic clove
7 ounces mushrooms
1 bunch parsley
2 tablespoons (¼ stick) butter
3 sprigs marjoram
Salt and freshly ground black pepper
Juice of ½ lemon
1 cup crème fraîche or sour cream
2 tablespoons olive oil
½ cup hot meat broth

4 servings
420 calories per serving
Preparation time: about 1½ hours

Wash zucchini under cold running water; dry. Trim ends and halve zucchini lengthwise.

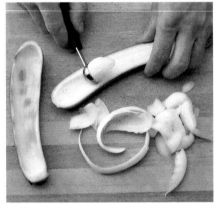

• Carefully scoop out zucchini flesh without piercing through skin or ends; this is most easily done with a melon baller or teaspoon. Finely chop scooped-out zucchini.

• Using a small, sharp knife, trim away any membranes or tubules from livers. Pat livers dry with paper towels and dice finely.
• Mince onion and garlic. Clean mushrooms. Rinse parsley and shake dry; chop along with mushrooms.
• Melt about ⅔ of butter in large skillet. Add onion and garlic and cook until translucent. Stir in mushrooms, parsley and chopped zucchini and cook until liquid has evaporated.
• Rinse marjoram and blot dry. Finely chop leaves.

• Push mushroom mixture to one side of skillet. Melt remaining butter on cleared surface of skillet over gentle heat. Add livers and cook until lightly browned outside but still pink inside. Blend well with mushroom mixture and season with marjoram, salt, pepper and a few drops of lemon juice.

• Stir in about 2 tablespoons crème fraîche.
• Preheat oven to 400°F. Warm a rectangular baking dish in oven.
• Stuff zucchini halves with liver mixture.
• Brush heated baking dish with part of olive oil and arrange zucchini halves in dish. Drizzle stuffing with remaining oil; pour hot broth and remaining lemon juice into dish. Cover and bake 20 minutes.
• Transfer zucchini to heated serving dish and keep warm.
• Pour cooking liquid into wide saucepan, whisk in remaining crème fraîche and boil down over high heat to creamy sauce consistency. Season with salt and pepper and pour over and around zucchini. Serve with boiled potatoes or rice.

Variation: Zucchini with Herbed Bread Stuffing

Hollow out zucchini halves as in master recipe; chop zucchini flesh. Trim crusts from 3 stale rolls; cut rolls into tiny cubes. Mince 2 onions and 3 to 4 garlic cloves; finely chop 2 bunches parsley and ½ bunch dill. Heat 1 to 2 tablespoons olive oil in large skillet. Add onions and chopped zucchini and cook until translucent. Stir in garlic and herbs, cook briefly, season with salt and pepper and remove from heat. Cool slightly, then mix in 1 egg yolk and 3 to 5 minced anchovy fillets, depending on their saltiness. Mince 1 ounce shelled walnuts and stir into filling with 3 tablespoons freshly grated Parmesan and ½ cup grated Gruyère or Emmental cheeses. Stuff zucchini with this mixture and arrange in baking dish brushed with olive oil. Generously sprinkle stuffing with additional olive oil and pour about ½ cup hot chicken or beef broth into dish. Bake in preheated 400°F oven until zucchini is tender, about 20 to 30 minutes depending on size. Pour liquid into large saucepan and boil down until thickened to sauce consistency; cover zucchini and keep warm. Season sauce with salt and pepper and pour around zucchini.

Tip: This stuffing can be given even more flavor if you start by cooking 3 ounces chopped bacon over low heat until fat is rendered, then add oil, onion and remaining ingredients and proceed as directed. You can also vary the herbs and cheese. For example, Gouda can be substituted for Gruyère or mozzarella for both cheeses, and instead of the herbs called for you may wish to use oregano and thyme or basil.

Outwardly, zucchini resembles cucumbers much more than it does the gourds and pumpkins to which it is actually related. But the first taste reveals its family likeness to the other squashes: like them, it has a mild flavor that readily harmonizes with many different herbs, spices and stuffings. You can, for example, stuff zucchini with the fillings given in this book for stuffed peppers, crepes, or pork tenderloin (see Index); or stuff them with leftover meat, chopped and mixed with a bit of cream or cheese.

Braised Oyster Mushrooms

Until a few years ago oyster mushrooms were a rarity prized by gourmets for their wild flavor and aroma, which are somewhat reminiscent of veal. Today these mushrooms can be found in many well-stocked markets and greengrocers. Oyster mushrooms can be used in any mushroom recipe, but taste best when braised or grilled.

| 2¼ pounds oyster mushrooms |
| 1 shallot |
| 3 garlic cloves |
| 3 tablespoons olive oil |
| 1 generous tablespoon butter |
| Salt and freshly ground white pepper |
| Juice of ½ lemon |
| 2 sprigs thyme |
| 1 bunch parsley, chopped |

4 servings
190 calories per serving
Preparation time: about 30 minutes

Separate and clean oyster mushrooms, lifting out any bits of straw or debris from cap or gills with a paring knife.
• Briefly rinse mushrooms in batches in strainer; do not soak, or they will absorb water and lose flavor. Drain well or, better, dry individually with towel (this is the best procedure for all mushrooms, whether wild or cultivated).

• Trim away woody stems and cut up mushroom caps. Finely chop shallot; chop garlic.
• Heat olive oil in large skillet; add butter and allow to melt. Add shallot and garlic and cook over medium heat until translucent. Stir in mushrooms and cook, stirring, until all moisture has evaporated. Season with salt and white pepper.

• Sprinkle lemon juice over mushrooms.
• Rinse thyme sprigs and shake thoroughly dry. Strip leaves from stems, mix with chopped parsley and stir into oysters. Cook over medium heat for 2 more minutes; serve hot.

Variation:
Chanterelles with Eggs

Clean and briefly rinse 14 ounces fresh chanterelles; pat dry. Halve or quarter large mushrooms. Finely chop 1 medium onion. Wash, shake dry and finely chop ½ bunch parsley. Melt 2 tablespoons (¼ stick) butter in large skillet. Add onion and parsley and stir over medium heat until onion is translucent. Add mushrooms and cook until all moisture has evaporated. Season with salt and freshly ground white pepper. Whisk 4 eggs with 2 to 4 tablespoons heavy cream. Pour over chanterelles and cook over medium heat until set, stirring once or twice.

Mushrooms in Cream

Mushrooms in cream are a supremely elegant side dish, but they might be even better served in double quantities with noodles or dumplings as a main course. If possible, add a few porcini or chanterelles to intensify the flavor.

Equally delicious as entree or side dish.

1 generous pound mixed fresh mushrooms: cultivated white, cèpes or porcini, chanterelles, straw mushrooms, shiitake, etc.
1 large onion
1 bunch parsley
3 tablespoons butter
1 tablespoon all-purpose flour
1 cup heavy cream
Salt and freshly ground white pepper

4 servings
350 calories per serving
Preparation time: about 1 hour

C lean mushrooms; if necessary, rinse and dry thoroughly. (Do not soak mushrooms or they will lose flavor.) Cut into thin slices.
• Mince onion; finely chop parsley.
• Melt butter in wide saucepan or Dutch oven. Add onion and cook, stirring frequently, until translucent. Add mushrooms and cook, stirring occasionally, until all moisture has evaporated, about 5 minutes.
• Sprinkle flour over mushrooms and blend in well. Cook, stirring, until flour mixture foams slightly at bottom of pan.

• Add parsley and cream and stir briskly to blend cream and flour so that flour does not brown.
• Cook mushrooms over gentle heat another 5 to 10 minutes, depending on size and variety. Season with salt and white pepper. Serve immediately.

Vegetable Soufflé

This is flavored with lots of fresh seasonal vegetables and enriched with meat.

1 generous pound broccoli
1 generous pound kohlrabi
1 generous pound baby carrots
8 to 9 ounces pickled tongue
5 ounces Gouda cheese
1 onion
1 garlic clove
Salt
2 tablespoons (¼ stick) butter
1 tablespoon all-purpose flour
1 cup reserved vegetable cooking water
½ cup heavy cream
3 egg yolks
Freshly grated nutmeg
Freshly ground white pepper
2 egg whites
Butter for baking dish

4 servings
630 calories per serving
Preparation time: about 1¼ hours

Trim tough leaves and woody stems from broccoli. Separate broccoli into florets; peel stems and cut away ends.

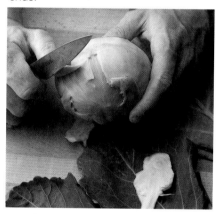

• Remove leaves from kohlrabi. Rinse, drain and finely chop tender young leaves and set aside for sauce. Peel bulb with sharp knife; trim away any woody parts, particularly at root end. (Buy the youngest kohlrabi you can find; they will be more tender than large older specimens and will have less waste.) Quarter and slice kohlrabi bulbs.
• Scrape carrots by holding each firmly at base of stalk and scraping off skin from top to bottom with knife held diagonally. Trim stems and root ends and wash carrots.

• Cut tongue into fine strips or squares. Grate cheese. Finely chop onion; chop garlic and crush with a little salt.
• Bring large pot of salted water to rapid boil.
• Drop broccoli florets into boiling water and blanch 2 minutes over high heat. Remove with skimmer and plunge into ice water. (Blanching and quick chilling will preserve broccoli's bright green color.) Blanch carrots 10 minutes and kohlrabi slices 7 minutes, plunging each into ice water. Drain all vegetables well.
• Reserve 1 cup vegetable cooking water for sauce; discard remainder or set aside for making soup.
• Adjust oven rack to second position from bottom and preheat oven to 400°F.
• Melt 1 tablespoon butter in large deep saucepan over medium heat; butter should foam lightly but not brown. Add onion and cook, stirring frequently, until translucent but not browned. Add garlic.

• Sprinkle in flour and cook over medium heat, stirring constantly, until mixture is light yellow.
• Pour in ¼ cup vegetable cooking liquid, whisking hard to prevent lumps from forming. When liquid is completely incorporated, pour in remaining ¾ cup cooking water.

• Continue to whisk sauce until smooth. Cook over low heat 10 minutes (all flour-based sauces must cook long enough to remove any raw flour taste).
• Whisk in cream and remove from heat.

• Pour a small amount of sauce into a bowl and whisk in egg yolks. Whisk yolk mixture back into remaining sauce.
• Add about ⅔ of grated Gouda to sauce and stir until melted. Add chopped kohlrabi leaves. Season sauce with salt, nutmeg and white pepper. Let cool slightly.
• Beat egg whites with a pinch of salt until stiff. Gently fold into sauce.
• Butter a soufflé mold or baking dish. Add vegetables, tongue and sauce in layers, ending with sauce. Sprinkle with remaining grated cheese and dot with remaining butter.
• Bake soufflé until cheese is melted and top is nicely browned, about 30 minutes. Serve immediately.

Variation:
Quick Vegetable Soufflé

Scrub 1 generous pound salsify under running water; peel. Drop peeled roots into cold water acidulated with a bit of fresh lemon juice to prevent discoloration. Cut roots into 2-inch pieces and cook in boiling salted water until tender, about 20 minutes. Remove with skimmer and drain well. Blanch 1 generous pound chopped cabbage in same water for 3 minutes; plunge into ice water and drain. Cut 10 to 11 ounces boiled ham into strips and sauté in butter with 1 chopped onion until onion is translucent. Mix 1 scant cup crème fraîche or sour cream, ½ cup milk, 1 egg, 2 tablespoons chopped fresh parsley and 1 cup grated cheese. Layer vegetables, ham mixture and sauce in greased baking dish, ending with sauce. Top with ½ cup additional grated cheese and dot with butter. Bake as directed in master recipe.

In preparing this soufflé let yourself be inspired by whatever vegetables are freshest and most appealing at the market. The dish's preparation takes some time, but it's very simple: the pre-cooked vegetables are layered in a baking dish with tongue—or with sausage, ham or bacon—and are then covered with a rich cheese sauce and baked. You can also make use of many types of leftovers in this manner. In the case of leftover cooked vegetables, the baking time should be shortened somewhat so that they do not become too soft: Simply raise the oven temperature so that the soufflé browns quickly.

Potato-Leek Gratin

Simple to assemble, but takes a while to cook.

1 to 2 garlic cloves
3 tablespoons butter
1 generous pound baking potatoes
2 leeks
Salt and freshly ground black pepper
Freshly grated nutmeg
3 cups heavy cream
⅓ cup grated Gruyère or Emmental cheese
1 ounce (about ¼ cup) freshly grated Parmesan cheese

4 servings
870 calories per serving
Preparation time: about 1½ hours

Halve garlic cloves. Carefully rub bottom and sides of gratin dish with cut sides of garlic, then grease dish with part of butter.

• Peel and wash potatoes; cut into even ⅛-inch slices with knife or vegetable slicer. Spread slices on paper towels to absorb excess moisture.
• Position rack to center of oven and preheat oven to 425°F.

• Trim roots and tough green leaves from leeks. Slit leeks lengthwise down to about an inch from root end and spread

layers under cold running water to wash out all grit. Slice leeks into thin rings.

• Fill prepared gratin dish with alternate crosswise strips of potato and leek: First arrange two layers of potato slices across end of pan to overlap like roof tiles, then add a row of leek, and continue to alternate down length of dish, ending each strip of vegetable slices about ¼ inch in from side of dish. Season vegetables with salt, pepper and nutmeg.

• Gradually pour in cream, allowing it to fill spaces between vegetable slices; shake dish gently so that vegetables are evenly covered.
• Sprinkle evenly with grated cheeses and dot with remaining butter.
• Bake gratin until potatoes are tender, 45 to 60 minutes. Cooking time will depend on type of potatoes used; test for doneness by piercing a few slices with a fork from time to time. If top of gratin browns too quickly, cover lightly with aluminum foil.
• Serve piping hot. Potato-leek gratin is excellent as an accompaniment for lamb dishes and grilled beef; it can also be served as a first course, or as a main dish if paired with a green salad.

Variation: Kohlrabi Gratin

Peel 1¼ pounds tender young kohlrabi; halve or quarter, depending on size of bulbs. Cut into slices about ⅛ inch thick. Sprinkle lightly with salt and let stand for 5 minutes, then pat each slice thoroughly dry with paper towels. Generously butter a gratin dish. Layer kohlrabi slices in dish, seasoning each layer with salt and pepper. Mix 1 cup heavy cream and ½ cup milk and pour over kohlrabi. Bake in preheated 375°F. oven for about 45 minutes. Serve with roast beef or pork or with lamb chops.

Variation: Fennel Gratin

Trim, wash and halve 3 medium fennel bulbs. Blanch in boiling salted water for 10 minutes. Drain well and arrange in a greased gratin dish. Season with salt, pepper, some finely chopped garlic and a few anise seeds; pour 1 cup whisked crème fraîche over. Sprinkle with ⅓ cup mixed freshly grated Parmesan and Gouda cheese. Bake in preheated 400°F. oven for about 35 minutes. Serve with grilled lamb or beef or with fish.

Variation: Gratin with Apple

Peel and core 4 medium apples (Gravensteins are especially good). Thinly slice and immediately sprinkle with fresh lemon juice to prevent discoloration. Butter a gratin dish and add apple slices in layers, sprinkling each layer with a bit more lemon juice. Whisk 1 cup crème fraîche with 1 cup heavy cream, pour over apples and bake in preheated 425°F. oven for about 20 minutes. Serve with game or pork.

A good *gratin* is tender inside, crisp and browned on top. The most famous dish of the type is probably *Gratin Dauphinoise*, which consists of potatoes covered with heavy cream, a mixture of heavy cream and crème fraîche, or occasionally with a lower-calorie combination of cream and milk. It can also be made with a mixture of milk and eggs. This potato-leek version is one of many possible variations.

Spaetzle

A beloved Swabian specialty.

Spaetzle made only with whole eggs and egg yolks have an especially nutty flavor and retain a firm texture after cooking. If part of the yolk is replaced with water the *spaetzle* will be softer. The exact quantity of liquid will vary according to the size and freshness of the eggs and the moisture content of the flour.

2 cups all-purpose flour
1 teaspoon salt
4 eggs
1½ teaspoons vegetable oil
1 to 3 egg yolks (or some cold water)
4 quarts salted water for cooking
1 tablespoon butter

4 servings
480 calories per serving
Preparation time: 45 to 60 minutes
Resting time: 30 minutes

Mix flour with salt, eggs, oil and enough egg yolk or cold water to form a very thick batter. Beat until bubbles appear on surface and batter pulls away from side of bowl. Let rest 30 minutes to let flour absorb moisture. If batter is too stiff after resting period, mix in a bit more yolk or water.
• Bring salted water to boil in large pot.
• Rinse a wooden cutting board and a large knife or metal spatula with cold water. Spread batter thinly on board in batches. Hold board diagonally over pot and scrape off narrow strips of batter

with knife directly into boiling water, dipping knife into cold water in between.
• As soon as *spaetzle* rise to surface of water, remove with skimmer or slotted spoon, drain and transfer to heated bowl. Keep warm until all batter is cooked.
• Melt (but do not brown) butter. Pour over *spaetzle* and toss lightly. Serve immediately.

Variation: Spinach *Spaetzle*

Sort and wash 5 ounces spinach; blanch in boiling salted water for 3 to 4 minutes. Plunge into ice water, drain, squeeze dry and chop finely. Combine spinach with 2 cups all-purpose flour, 2 to 3 eggs and 1 to 2 egg yolks. Season with salt and nutmeg and proceed as above.

Variation: Herb *Spaetzle*

Rinse, shake dry and finely chop 5 ounces fresh herbs (equal quantities of parsley, chervil, chives and tarragon are good). Mix with 2 cups all-purpose flour, 1 teaspoon salt, 3 eggs and additional egg yolks as needed (exact amount will depend on moisture content of herbs) to form thick batter. Proceed with recipe.

Variation: Liver *Spaetzle*

Combine 7 ounces puréed beef liver with 2¾ cups all-purpose flour, 3 eggs, 1 tablespoon chopped fresh parsley, ½ to 1 pressed garlic clove, 1 teaspoon dried marjoram, crushed, and salt and freshly ground black pepper. Proceed as for master recipe.

Cheese Spaetzle

The finished *spaetzle* can be kept warm in a 175°F oven while remaining batter is cooked; if you work slowly, reduce the oven temperature to 125°F so that *spaetzle* do not dry out and cheese does not toughen. If you will be serving a salad with this, prepare it ahead of time.

This *must* be served piping hot.

3½ cups all-purpose flour
2 teaspoons salt
1½ teaspoons vegetable oil
6 eggs
1 to 3 egg yolks (or some cold water)
4 large onions
5 tablespoons butter
4 quarts salted water for cooking
7 ounces Emmenthal cheese

4 servings
1025 calories per serving
Preparation time: about 1¼ hours

Mix flour with salt, oil, eggs and enough egg yolk or cold water to form a very thick batter. Beat until bubbles appear on surface and batter pulls away from side of bowl. Let rest 30 minutes to let flour absorb moisture. If batter is too stiff after resting period, mix in a bit more yolk or water.

• Meanwhile, slice onions into thin rings. Melt butter in large skillet and cook onions, stirring frequently, until brown.

• Bring salted water to boil in large pot. Preheat oven to 175°F.

• Shred Emmenthal.

• Rinse a wooden cutting board and large knife or metal spatula with cold water. Spread batter thinly on board in batches. Hold board diagonally over pot and scrape off narrow strips of batter with knife directly into boiling water, dipping knife into cold water in between.

• As soon as *spaetzle* rise to surface of water, remove with skimmer or slotted spoon, drain and layer with some of cheese in baking dish. Continue until all batter is cooked, covering dish and keeping finished *spaetzle* warm in oven.

• When all *spaetzle* have been added to baking dish, top with remaining cheese and hot cooked onions. Serve immediately.

Piquant Potato Salad

This tastes best served at room temperature.

2 egg yolks
2 teaspoons Dijon mustard
1 tablespoon fresh lemon juice
½ cup vegetable oil
2¼ pounds boiling potatoes
Salt and freshly ground black pepper
1 onion
1 dill pickle
1 tart apple
1 tablespoon drained capers
1 tablespoon plain yogurt
3 tablespoons pickle brine

4 servings
570 calories per serving
Preparation time: about 1 hour
Resting time: 30 minutes

For mayonnaise have egg yolks, mustard, lemon juice and oil at room temperature. (If ingredients are too cold or vary too widely in temperature, mayonnaise is likely to curdle.)
• Scrub potatoes well under cold running water.
• Pour cold water into large saucepan to depth of about 2 inches. Add potatoes, cover and bring to boil over high heat, then reduce heat to low and cook 25 to 30 minutes longer, depending on size and type of potato used. (Do not overcook or potatoes will fall apart when sliced. Test for doneness frequently by inserting the point of a paring knife into potatoes; they are done when they can be pierced easily but there is still a slight resistance at center.)

• For mayonnaise, place egg yolks in mixing bowl. Blend in salt to taste, pepper, mustard and lemon juice (this is best done with a whisk, but a portable mixer can also be used).

• When all ingredients are blended and smooth, start adding oil a drop at a time, whisking constantly. As oil is incorporated, begin adding remainder in a thin stream; be careful not to add too much oil at a time or the emulsion will separate and mayonnaise will curdle. If this should happen, mayonnaise can be rescued by whisking another egg yolk in a separate bowl and gradually whisking in curdled mayonnaise.
• When all oil is incorporated, test consistency of mayonnaise; it should be thick enough to cling to the blade of a knife. Season with salt and pepper.
• Plunge potatoes into ice water to make peeling easier.

• While potatoes are still warm, peel and cut into ¼-inch slices. (Potato salad should always be made with hot or warm potato slices, for the potato starch will not yet have congealed and slices will better absorb dressing.)
• Finely chop onion; sprinkle with salt to draw out some of juice and mellow onion's sharpness.
• Dice pickle. Quarter, core and peel apple; cut into small cubes.

• Gently mix potato slices, onion, pickle, apple and capers.

• Whisk yogurt and pickle brine into mayonnaise and toss with potato mixture. Cover and let stand 30 minutes. Taste and adjust seasoning before serving. Salad makes an excellent accompaniment to fried fish fillets, pork or veal cutlets and grilled chops.

Variation:
Bavarian Potato Salad

Scrub and cook 2¼ pounds boiling potatoes as in master recipe. Peel and slice potatoes while still warm. While potatoes cook, prepare dressing by whisking together 1 cup double-strength bouillon (from cubes), 1½ teaspoons sharp mustard, 2 tablespoons wine vinegar, salt, freshly ground black pepper and ¼ cup vegetable oil. Toss potato slices with dressing, 1 large chopped onion and 2 tablespoons snipped chives. Let stand 30 minutes before serving.

Using the right kind of potatoes is the alpha and omega of a good potato salad, for the cooked potatoes must be firm enough to slice without falling apart. Be sure to buy waxy boiling potatoes, not the baking varieties grown in Maine and Idaho.

Bacon Dumplings

In southern Germany and Austria, dumplings—whether made with potatoes, bread or flour—are perennially popular as a side dish. They are best suited to an entree served with sauce or gravy, since they lend themselves so well to dunking. In rustic cooking, dumplings are also a satisfying main dish.

Accompany with sauerkraut for a hearty meal.

| 10 day-old French or dinner rolls |
| 1½ cups milk |
| 7 ounces bacon |
| 1 medium onion |
| Salt |
| 1 bunch parsley, chopped |
| 3 eggs |

4 servings
740 calories per serving
Preparation time: about 40 minutes

Thinly slice rolls. Place slices in large bowl.
• Heat milk until lukewarm and pour evenly over roll slices. Lay round board or pot lid on top and weight it to keep bread submerged so that it softens evenly.
• Finely dice bacon, discarding any rind. Finely chop onion.
• Pour 4 quarts water into large pot. Add 2 tablespoons salt and bring to boil.
• Heat ungreased heavy skillet. Add bacon and cook, stirring, over medium heat until fat is rendered. As soon as bacon is surrounded by melted fat, stir in onion and parsley and cook until onion is translucent. Let mixture cool.
• Add eggs and bacon mixture to softened bread and blend well with moistened hands or with dough hook attachment of electric mixer. Season mixture with salt.

• With moistened hands form dough into dumplings and arrange on plate. Drop into slowly boiling water and simmer uncovered 10 to 15 minutes, carefully loosening any dumplings that stick to bottom of pan using a wooden spoon (dumplings will rise to surface when cooked).
• Lift cooked dumplings from water with skimmer or slotted spoon; drain well. Transfer to warmed serving bowl and serve right away. These are very good with sauerkraut or with mushrooms in cream.

Tip: Classic bread dumplings, or Semmelknödel, are prepared in the same way; omit bacon and add onion to dough without precooking.

Raw-Potato Dumplings

Yes, there are good potato dumpling mixes, but now and then you really should take the trouble to make them yourself. You'll find them easier than you'd expect. Use mealy baking potatoes; the waxy boiling varieties are not suitable for dumplings.

These take some time in the preparation, but when made from scratch they are a true delicacy.

2¼ pounds prepared baking potatoes
(weigh after peeling and trimming)
Vinegar
1 cup milk
1 tablespoon salt
Potato starch, if needed
1 French or dinner roll
2 tablespoons (¼ stick) butter

4 servings
480 calories per serving
Preparation time: about 1½ hours

Peel and wash potatoes; pat dry. Weigh as accurately as possible. Cook half (1 pound, 2 ounces) of potatoes in boiling salted water until tender. Grate remaining raw potatoes and sprinkle with vinegar.
• Spread grated potato in towel and squeeze as dry as possible, collecting juice in a bowl. Set juice aside to let starch settle out. Place potato shreds in mixing bowl.
• Bring milk to boil.
• Drain potatoes and mash or purée.

• Carefully pour off potato juice, leaving starch behind in bottom of bowl.
• Pour boiling milk over raw potatoes. Add mashed potatoes, potato starch and salt and blend into a firm, nonsticky dough.
• Moisten hands with cold water and form a test dumpling; cook in boiling salted water to see if it holds together. If dumpling falls apart, knead a bit of packaged potato starch into dough.
• While test dumpling cooks, finely dice roll and fry in butter until golden. Let cool.
• Form remaining dough into dumplings, filling each with a few bread cubes. Drop into boiling water and cook over high heat until water returns to boil. Reduce heat to low and continue cooking dumplings, uncovered or half covered, for 20 to 30 minutes. Drain well before serving.

Swiss *Rösti* Potatoes

A famous and beloved Swiss specialty.

As is true of so many regional specialties, there are about as many recipes for *Rösti* as there are families who prepare it. Some use cooked potatoes, some mix cooked and raw, and others swear that *Rösti* must only be made with raw potatoes. In any case, it is essential to use mealy baking potatoes.

| 1 pound, 10 ounces baking potatoes |
| Salt and freshly ground white pepper |
| Freshly grated nutmeg |
| 7 tablespoons (about) butter |
| ¼ bunch parsley |

4 servings
305 calories per serving
Preparation time: about 1 hour

Peel potatoes, rinse in cold water and pat thoroughly dry with paper towels. Shred into bowl on large holes of grater. Season potatoes with salt, white pepper and nutmeg.
• Melt a scant tablespoon of butter in heated skillet.
• Preheat oven to 175°F to keep cooked potatoes warm while cooking remainder.
• Remove about ¼ of potato mixture from bowl and press flat between palms of hands.
• Place pressed potato cake into hot butter and flatten into even, round disc with spatula. Cook for a few seconds over high heat, then reduce heat and

cook until potatoes are nearly done, about 10 to 15 more minutes.

• Slide potatoes onto pan lid and immediately increase heat under skillet to high. Melt another scant tablespoon butter in skillet and return potatoes to pan cooked side up. Again cook for several seconds over high heat, then reduce heat and cook *Rösti* 10 to 15 minutes.
• Drain potatoes quickly on several

layers of paper towel. Keep warm in oven while cooking remaining *Rösti*; arrange in single layer, not overlapping, to keep potatoes from softening.
• Rinse parsley and shake dry; chop finely.
• Transfer *Rösti* to heated serving plates or platter and serve garnished with parsley. Accompany with a large green or mixed salad.

Tip: *Rösti* becomes an elegant side dish when cooked in mini-portions and served with sautéed or broiled meats, saddle of venison, leg of lamb or other roasts. It is particularly flavorful if a bit of finely chopped onion, paper-thin bacon strips or coarsely shredded Emmenthal cheese is mixed in; in all of these cases a green salad is the best partner.

Raw-Potato Home Fries

In contrast to the usual home fries, which are frequently made with leftover cooked potatoes, this version is a delicacy with origins in rustic country cooking. The dish is often flavored with a bit of bacon or ham.

Altogether, a marvelous dish.

2¼ pounds boiling potatoes
6 tablespoons olive oil
2 large onions
1 to 2 garlic cloves
1 bunch chives
1 generous tablespoon butter
Salt and freshly ground white pepper
1 to 2 teaspoons caraway seed

4 servings
350 calories per serving
Preparation time: about 40 minutes

Peel and wash potatoes; cut into even slices with vegetable slicer. Arrange on thick layer of paper towel and pat dry with more towels.
• Heat olive oil in large skillet. Add potatoes and cook on all sides over high heat, stirring frequently.
• Halve onions and cut into strips. Mix into potatoes and sauté a few minutes over high heat, then reduce heat to medium and cook 20 minutes longer, stirring occasionally. Finely chop garlic. Wash chives and shake dry; snip finely.

• Cut butter into small pieces and gradually add to potatoes; let potatoes cook briefly in butter. (This final addition of butter lends a particularly appetizing flavor and aroma to the dish.) Season potatoes with garlic and generous quantities of salt and white pepper. Sprinkle with caraway and stir and cook a minute or two longer. Drain on paper towels if desired. Sprinkle with chives and serve immediately with sautéed or broiled meat of any kind; these home fries also make a complete meal when served with eggs and a green salad.

Real Vanilla Bavarian Cream

A mellow, creamy treat that will make you want to forget calories.

2 envelopes unflavored gelantin
½ cup cold water
2 cups milk
Pinch of salt
1 vanilla bean
5 egg yolks
½ cup sugar
2 cups heavy cream
1 envelope vanilla sugar or ¾ teaspoon vanilla extract

6 servings
450 calories per serving
Preparation time: about 1 hour
Chilling time: about 3 hours

Sprinkle gelatin over water and set aside to soften.
• Combine milk and salt in saucepan.
• Split vanilla bean lengthwise and scrape out seeds with tip of paring knife. Combine seeds and pod with milk and bring just to boil. Remove from heat and set aside to steep.
• Place egg yolks in another saucepan and whisk until light. Gradually add sugar and whisk until dissolved.
• Remove vanilla bean from milk. Place egg yolks over very low heat and immediately—before bottom of pan is hot—start whisking in milk a little at a time.
• Using a wooden spoon or spatula, stir mixture constantly until thickened and creamy; *do not boil* or yolks will curdle.

• Mixture has the right consistency when it coats spoon and no longer flows freely. (To test for proper thickness, blow lightly on surface; the mixture should show small circular waves resembling a rose. In fact, some European chefs refer to this stage as "cooked to the rose.")

• Stir softened gelatin into heated mixture. Continue to stir until gelatin is completely dissolved, heating gently if necessary.
• Half fill a large bowl with cold water; add 2 to 3 handfuls of ice cubes.

• Place a smaller bowl into bowl of ice water and pour in yolk mixture through strainer (this step is to eliminate any bits of undissolved gelatin or remnants of congealed egg white that would spoil dessert's smooth texture).
• Let mixture stand in ice water, stirring frequently, until cooled and thickened.

• Whip cream until soft peaks form, adding vanilla sugar or extract.
• As soon as yolk mixture is thickened enough that a spoon drawn across surface leaves a noticeable path, add whipped cream and blend very gently with whisk or spatula; do not agitate mixture more than necessary or it will deflate. It is also important that both mixtures be at about the same temperature: If yolks are too warm, whipped cream will melt, but if they are too cold they will be too stiff to blend smoothly. Refrigerate Bavarian cream until serving

time, stirring occasionally to keep it light and to prevent skin from forming on surface. Spoon into chilled individual dishes just before serving.

Tip: To avoid the possibility of curdling yolks, mixture may be cooked in double boiler top or metal bowl set over hot (not boiling) water.

Variation: Raspberry-Center Bavarian Cream

Combine about 1 pound, 5 ounces raspberries with ⅓ to ½ cup sugar (depending on sweetness of berries), 3 tablespoons raspberry *eau de vie* and a few drops of raspberry liqueur or kirsch. Cover and let stand a few minutes, then purée in blender or processor. Transfer to non-aluminum saucepan and warm over low heat until sugar is dissolved. Meanwhile, soften 1 envelope unflavored gelatin in ¼ cup cold water. Add to warmed berry purée and stir until gelatin is dissolved; cool. Prepare Bavarian cream as in master recipe, using 2½ to 3 envelopes unflavored gelatin. When chilled but not quite set, fold about ⅓ of Bavarian into raspberry mixture. Transfer remaining plain Bavarian to a round-bottomed bowl. Spoon raspberry cream into pastry bag fitted with large plain tip; insert into center of plain cream and squeeze out raspberry mixture to form a pink "core" in the vanilla cream. Chill 6 to 8 hours. Invert onto round platter to serve.

Bavarian cream, or *Crème Bavaroise*, can be prepared and served in countless ways. It is wonderful when flavored with walnuts, almonds, coffee, cocoa, chocolate, or various liquors or liqueurs; you can also add puréed or chopped fruit and/or serve the Bavarian with various sauces of your choice. This recipe results in a light, loose Bavarian. If you want a dessert that can be unmolded, add another half to whole envelope of gelatin; the same applies if you will be adding chopped or puréed fruit.

Griessflammeri (Molded Farina Pudding)

Prepare this the day before serving.

This wonderfully light, delicate dessert has nothing whatever in common with the bland farina cereal that everyone remembers from childhood. Here the neutral farina is flavored with lemon and almonds; other possibilities are liquors, liqueurs and different kinds of nuts.

2 cups milk
Salt
¼ lemon
1 sugar cube
2 tablespoons sugar
7 tablespoons farina
2 eggs
¼ cup finely chopped blanched almonds

4 servings
290 calories per serving
Preparation time: about 40 minutes
Chilling time: about 12 hours

Combine milk and pinch of salt in deep saucepan. Rub lemon peel with sugar cube to absorb as much color and flavor as possible; drop sugar cube into milk.
• Bring milk to boil. Add sugar and farina and return to boil, stirring.
• Reduce heat to very low and cook farina 10 minutes, stirring frequently to prevent scorching. (Use a flame tamer or asbestos pad over burner if you have one.) Remove mixture from heat.

• Separate eggs. Briskly stir some of hot farina mixture into yolks, then return to saucepan and blend well.

• Combine egg whites and pinch of salt and beat to stiff peaks. Stir into hot farina mixture (you need not be as careful as usual not to deflate whites, since the heat of the farina will liquefy them somewhat anyway).
• Stir in almonds. Taste pudding and add more sugar if necessary.
• Rinse a 4-cup mold or 4 individual

bowls with cold water. Turn pudding into mold and smooth top. Cover and chill about 12 hours.
• Moisten a plate with cold water to keep pudding from sticking to it. Invert pudding onto plate and serve. Thick, sweetened raspberry juice or stewed sour cherries make delicious sauces.

Variation:
Vanilla Pudding with Fruit

Combine 2 cups milk, pinch of salt, lemon peel (grated as in master recipe), seeds scraped from 1 vanilla bean and 2½ tablespoons sugar in saucepan and bring to boil. Meanwhile, stir ¼ cup cornstarch into enough cold water to make a thin paste. Stir into saucepan and return to boil. Remove from heat and cool slightly. Stir some of pudding mixture into 2 beaten egg yolks; return to saucepan and blend well. Stir in 2 stiffly beaten egg whites. Layer pudding with crumbled macaroons and well-drained stewed prunes in individual serving bowls. Chill thoroughly and garnish each serving with a dollop of whipped cream. This pudding is not unmolded.

Crème Brûlée

Crème brûlée means "burnt cream," but this is a charmless name for such a splendid and delicate dessert. Its special appeal lies in the combination of creamy, ice-cold custard and crisp, still-hot caramel topping.

Simply irresistible.

2 cups heavy cream
1 vanilla bean
5 egg yolks
3 tablespoons sugar
3 tablespoons orange liqueur
½ orange

6 servings
585 calories per serving
Preparation time: about 1½ hours
Chilling time: 4 to 6 hours

Pour cream into saucepan and place over medium heat until heated through; do not boil.

- Split vanilla bean lengthwise and scrape out seeds with tip of paring knife. Add seeds and pod to cream.
- Combine egg yolks with a scant half of sugar and all of orange liqueur. Beat until light and fluffy.
- Remove colored peel from orange half in paper-thin slices using vegetable peeler or sharp knife. Cut into very fine julienne and add to yolk mixture.
- Bring kettle of water to boil. Preheat oven to 350°F.
- Remove vanilla bean from cream. Pour cream into yolk mixture, whisking constantly.
- Line bottom of roasting pan with several layers of paper towel.
- Divide cream mixture among 6 individual soufflé dishes, leaving about ¾ inch between top of cream and top of dishes. Arrange in roasting pan without touching.
- Pour enough boiling water into pan to come halfway up sides of dishes. Bake 1 hour, covering with a sheet of aluminum foil (pierced with a number of holes) as soon as surface of cream starts to brown.
- Remove dishes from water bath and let cool. Chill 4 to 6 hours.
- Preheat broiler. Sprinkle remaining sugar over custards and broil until golden brown, watching carefully to prevent burning. Serve immediately.

Steamed Hazelnut Pudding

So light and delicate that it melts in the mouth.

Steamed puddings, with plum pudding being the best-known example, are English in origin. They were already known in other parts of Europe, however, by the end of the 17th century.

1 vanilla bean
⅓ cup sugar
1 generous tablespoon butter
3 ounces hazelnuts
3 egg yolks
2 tablespoons crème de cacao
2 egg whites
Pinch of salt
¼ cup all-purpose flour
Pinch of baking powder
1 cup flaked coconut
Butter for mold
1 tablespoon fine dry breadcrumbs

6 servings
224 calories per serving
Preparation time: about 1½ hours

Split vanilla bean lengthwise and scrape out seeds with tip of paring knife. Combine seeds with ¼ cup sugar.
• Preheat oven to 425°F.
• Melt butter over very low heat; cool to lukewarm.
• Spread hazelnuts on rimmed baking sheet. Toast in oven for 10 minutes, or until skins split.

• Transfer hazelnuts to kitchen towel and rub off skins. Let nuts cool to room temperature.
• Finely grate hazelnuts using rotary grater. Set 1 tablespoon grated nuts aside for sprinkling over mold.
• Combine egg yolks and crème de cacao and beat until foamy. Gradually add vanilla sugar and beat until thick and creamy.

• Combine egg whites and salt and beat until stiff peaks form, gradually adding remaining sugar. Slide egg whites out onto yolk mixture.
• Mix flour with baking powder, ground hazelnuts and coconut. Sprinkle over egg whites and fold together lightly.
• Pour melted butter over batter in thin stream and fold in carefully.
• Butter a 1-quart covered pudding mold. Mix breadcrumbs with reserved ground hazelnuts and sprinkle evenly over inside of mold.
• Turn batter into mold, spreading evenly (mold should be only ¾ full, as mixture will expand during steaming).
• Cover mold and place in narrow, deep saucepan. Add enough boiling water to pan to come ¾ up sides of mold. Simmer over low heat about 1 hour.
• Remove mold from water bath and uncover. Let stand about 2 minutes to allow steam to escape, then invert pudding onto plate. Serve hot for dessert or at room temperature in place of coffee-cake. Accompany with chocolate sauce if you wish.

Rote Grütze

A beloved German specialty, *Rote Grütze* is one of those simple dishes that appeals to a sweet tooth of any age. It is best when served ice cold, so you should prepare it at least six hours before serving to give it plenty of time in the refrigerator.

A wonderfully refreshing warm-weather dessert.

1 pound, 10 ounces fresh blackberries, strawberries, raspberries, red currants and blueberries, mixed

1 cup fruity dry red wine

3 tablespoons cornstarch

¼ cup sugar

1 piece of lemon peel (colored part only)

4 servings
210 calories per serving
Preparation time: about 30 minutes
Chilling time: about 6 hours

Rinse berries in cold water and drain thoroughly. Remove stems and hulls. Quarter strawberries.

• Stir together 3 tablespoons wine and cornstarch to make smooth paste.

• Combine remaining wine with sugar and lemon peel in large non-aluminum saucepan and bring to boil.

• Stir in cornstarch mixture and simmer over low heat 5 minutes. Discard lemon peel. Add berries to liquid and return to boil. Divide pudding among 4 serving dishes, cover and chill. Serve with chilled heavy cream.

Variation: Sour Cherry Jelly

Wash, drain and pit 10 to 11 ounces sour cherries. Combine 3 cups dry red wine, 6 tablespoons sugar and 1 piece of lime peel in non-aluminum saucepan and bring to boil. Add cherries and simmer over low heat 10 minutes. Discard lime peel. Purée cherries in processor, blender or food mill. Soften 2 envelopes unflavored gelatin in ½ cup cold water. Add to hot cherry puree and stir until gelatin is dissolved, heating gently if necessary. Rinse mold with cold water and add fruit puree. Chill until set.

Chocolate Mousse

The perfect conclusion to a festive dinner.

¼ cup double-strength coffee or espresso

7 ounces bittersweet or semisweet chocolate

½ cup (1 stick) unsalted butter

4 eggs

2 tablespoons sugar

Pinch of salt

1 cup heavy cream (optional)

6 servings
420 calories per serving
Preparation time: about 40 minutes

Gently heat coffee. Break chocolate into pieces and place in small saucepan.

- Pour hot water into larger saucepan and place over low heat. Set pan of chocolate into water and let stand until melted.
- Melt butter over low heat.

- Separate eggs. Place yolks in metal bowl; refrigerate whites.
- Half-fill large saucepan with hot water and place over medium heat. Set bowl of egg yolks over water and add coffee and sugar. Beat with whisk or portable mixer until sugar is dissolved and mixture is thick and creamy; it is the right consistency when the whisk leaves a visible path when drawn across the surface. Regulate heat under water bath so that water stays hot but does not boil, or yolks may curdle.

- Whisk in melted butter in a thin stream; continue whisking until butter is completely incorporated and mixture is smooth.
- Whisk in chocolate a tablespoon or so at a time. When mixture is dark brown and very thick, remove bowl from water bath.

- Whisk chocolate cream until cool; to speed the process, set bowl into larger bowl of ice water.
- Combine egg whites and salt and beat until stiff enough that a knife blade inserted into whites leaves a visible cut. Gently whisk egg whites into chocolate mixture (do not use mixer; it will deflate whites and make mousse heavy). Divide mousse among 6 individual dishes and chill until serving time.

- Mousse can also be served without the addition of egg whites; it will be thick and slightly flowing. In this case it can be served as soon as it is removed from ice water bath, without further chilling.

Variation:
White Chocolate Mousse

Melt 7 ounces white chocolate over hot (not boiling) water. While chocolate melts, melt ½ cup (1 stick) unsalted butter in small saucepan over low heat; do not let it color. Carefully skim off white foam that accumulates on surface. Pour melted clarified butter into another saucepan, leaving behind the white milk solids at bottom. Keep melted chocolate and clarified butter warm. Separate 4 eggs. Combine yolks with 3 tablespoons Amaretto liqueur in metal bowl and place over hot water bath; refrigerate whites. Beat yolks with whisk or portable mixer until light and creamy; they are the right consistency when the whisk leaves a visible path when drawn across the surface. Pour in warm clarified butter in a thin stream; continue whisking until butter is completely incorporated and mixture is smooth. Whisk in white chocolate a tablespoon or so at a time. Combine egg whites and a pinch of salt and beat until stiff. Fold carefully into chocolate mixture. Divide mousse among individual serving dishes. Toast 1 tablespoon sliced almonds in ungreased heavy small skillet until golden. Sprinkle over each serving of mousse. Garnish with ½ cup heavy cream, whipped to soft peaks.

There is such an enormous number of recipes for chocolate mousse that it's no longer possible to point to one "classic" or "definitive" version. Some chefs prepare a mousse that is a veritable calorie bomb, dark, dense and nougat-like in texture. Others prefer to lighten theirs with whipped egg whites and cream. In spite of its melting delicacy, this mousse is quite rich. Serve it as the crowning finale to an elegant meal.

Tiramisù

The main ingredient of this rich Italian dessert—whose name means "lift me up"—is mascarpone, a fresh cream cheese from Lombardy. Always use espresso in preparing this; lighter roast coffee will not give the dessert nearly as good a flavor.

This must be refrigerated at least eight hours, preferably overnight.

4 egg yolks

½ cup sugar

1 generous pound mascarpone, at room temperature

32 crisp ladyfingers or *savoiardi* biscuits

1½ cups cold espresso

Unsweetened cocoa powder

8 servings
440 calories per serving
Preparation time: about 30 minutes
Chilling time: at least 8 hours

Beat egg yolks until very light, gradually adding sugar. Beat until sugar is dissolved and mixture is nearly white. Gradually add mascarpone and beat until smooth and creamy.
• Lay half of cookies side by side in bottom of square dish. Slowly drizzle or brush with half of espresso, letting biscuits absorb it as evenly as possible. Be sure espresso is completely cold or it will soften biscuits excessively.

• Spread cookies with half of mascarpone cream, smoothing top and filling spaces between cookies as much as possible.
• Top with remaining biscuits and espresso; spread with remaining mascarpone.
• Sift a thin layer of cocoa lightly over top. Refrigerate *tiramisù* at least 8 hours, preferably overnight.

• Just before serving, sift a bit more cocoa lightly over top. Cut pudding into 8 equal pieces and lift carefully out of dish with wide spatula. Serve with a cup of espresso and, if you wish, a glass of brandy or *grappa*.

**Variation:
Brandied *Tiramisù***

Some Italian restaurants serve a liquor-spiked *tiramisù*. Mix espresso with about ⅓ cup brandy and, if you wish, a bit of powdered sugar and Amaretto liqueur. Proceed as directed in master recipe.

Zuppa Romana

Leave enough time for this to chill thoroughly before serving.

No one will know what you mean if you order *zuppa romana* in Italy, for there it's known as *zuppa inglese*—probably not because the English invented the dessert, but because the custard that gives *zuppa inglese* its luscious creaminess and flavor is *crème anglaise* or "English Cream."

3 eggs

1 cup minus 2 tablespoons sugar

½ teaspoon vanilla extract

5 tablespoons cornstarch

½ cup all-purpose flour

2 cups milk

1 vanilla bean, split lengthwise and seeds scraped

Pinch of salt

4 egg yolks

⅔ cup herbal liqueur or Marsala

5 ounces chopped candied fruit

2 cups cream, whipped to soft peaks

8 servings
560 calories per serving
Preparation time: about 1 hour
Chilling time: about 3 hours

Preheat oven to 350°F. Separate eggs. Beat yolks with 6 tablespoons sugar and vanilla extract until very light.

- Beat whites until stiff; slide onto yolk mixture. Set aside 1½ teaspoons cornstarch. Mix rest with 4½ tablespoons flour, sprinkle over egg whites; fold in. Spread batter in 9- to 10-inch springform pan, greased on bottom; bake until golden, about 20 minutes. Cool.
- For custard, heat milk, vanilla bean seeds, salt; do not boil.
- Combine egg yolks with ½ cup sugar and beat until very light. Blend in remaining flour and reserved 1½ teaspoons cornstarch. Gradually pour in heated milk, beating constantly. Return mixture to pan and bring to boil, stirring. When custard is thick, set pan in ice water; stir frequently until cooled.
- Cut biscuit into strips and use to line bottom of shallow dish; sprinkle with liqueur. Top with layer of custard, then candied fruit. Repeat layers until all ingredients are used, ending with biscuits. Cover with cream, garnish with fruit and chill.

Charlotte Royale

An attractive addition to a dessert buffet.

Cake:
4 egg yolks
3 tablespoons cold water
6 tablespoons sugar
1 envelope vanilla sugar or ½ teaspoon vanilla extract
4 egg whites
Pinch of salt
1 cup minus 2 tablespoons all-purpose flour
Butter for pan
Sugar for sprinkling cake
1 jar (about 16 ounces) red currant jelly

Custard:
2 envelopes unflavored gelatin
½ cup cold water
3 egg yolks
½ cup sugar
Juice of 2 lemons
1 cup full-bodied dry white wine
2 to 3 tablespoons Armagnac or Cognac
3 egg whites
Pinch of salt
1 cup heavy cream
1 envelope vanilla sugar or 1½ teaspoons vanilla extract

8 servings
490 calories per serving
Preparation time: about 1 hour
Chilling time: about 6 hours

Position rack in center of oven and preheat oven to 400°F.
• For cake, combine egg yolks and water in mixing bowl and beat until very light and foamy, gradually adding about ⅔ of sugar and all of vanilla sugar or extract. Continue beating until mixture is nearly white and sugar is dissolved.
• Beat egg whites with salt until stiff; gradually beat in remaining sugar.

• Slide egg whites out onto yolk mixture, sift flour over and fold together carefully.
• Line 15 × 10-inch jelly roll pan with parchment paper, folding margins of paper up at ends of pan to keep batter from flowing underneath. Lightly butter paper.

• Spread batter evenly in prepared pan. Immediately place in oven and bake until golden but not hard or dry, about 12 minutes.
• Spread clean kitchen towel on work surface and sprinkle with sugar.
• Melt currant jelly in saucepan over very low heat, stirring until smooth.
• Invert cake onto towel; moisten parchment paper with cold water and peel off.
• Immediately spread cake with jelly and roll up starting from one short end: Bend end of cake over jelly, then lift towel and roll remainder of cake using towel as aid. Wrap rolled cake in towel and let cool.
• For custard, sprinkle gelatin over cold water and let stand until softened.
• Combine egg yolks with about ⅔ of sugar and all of lemon juice and wine and beat until mixture is light and foamy and sugar is dissolved.

• Transfer gelatin to small saucepan and stir over low heat until dissolved. Remove from heat and let stand, stirring frequently, until cooled to same temperature as egg mixture.
• Blend some of egg mixture into gelatin, then pour back into remaining egg mixture, whisking hard. Whisk in Armagnac or Cognac and chill.
• Meanwhile, beat egg whites with salt until stiff. Gradually beat in remaining sugar. Combine cream and vanilla sugar or extract and beat until stiff.
• As soon as custard has thickened enough that a spoon drawn across surface leaves a visible path, fold in egg whites and cream. Refrigerate for a short while.

• Cut rolled cake into slices about ¼ to ⅜ inch thick. Line a smooth, rounded bowl with cake slices, reserving leftovers for snacks.

• As pudding is beginning to set, ladle into cake-lined bowl. Chill charlotte 4 to 5 hours. To serve, invert onto round platter and cut into wedges.

There is a wide assortment of classic charlottes—warm and cold, simple and elaborate—but this "regal" version is surely one of the finest. Even better known is charlotte russe, which is somewhat quicker to assemble because its outer layer is composed of ladyfingers. It can be filled with the same custard used for Charlotte Royale, or you may use the vanilla Bavarian on pages 104/105. Some charlottes have a fruit custard filling; still others use cookie wafers, plain cake strips or even slices of white bread for lining the mold.

Menus

Every good menu must be carefully planned, and it is the intention of this book— with its detailed instructions, step-by-step photos and explicit timing suggestions—to help make the planning a snap.

With roast pork, for example, an excellent first course is clear broth (prepared according to the recipe on page 10) with raw egg yolk and fresh herbs, with narrow strips of crepe (recipe on page 83) or with liver *spaetzle* (page 96). With stuffed chicken, try a first course of fresh figs or melon with prosciutto or another imported raw-cured ham. There are a thousand and one possibilities; decide on a particular dish according to what is fresh and seasonal in the market. With imagination and very little time you'll be able to work culinary sorcery that will surprise you: a few stalks of fresh asparagus with béarnaise sauce (page 42), assorted raw vegetables or cooked artichokes dipped in homemade herb mayonnaise (page 98), dandelion greens in spicy vinaigrette with crisp bacon bits, or avocado halves sprinkled with black pepper and dry Sherry or Port—all make wonderful starters. You can likewise put marvelous desserts on the table at a moment's notice: ice cream with, for instance, fresh or stewed fruit, macaroons or waffle cookies, hot chocolate or other sauces—and then there's always plain ice cream, perfumed with a bit of liqueur or fruit brandy. If you have a bit more time, whip up some paper-thin crepes (page 83) and fill them with jam or sweetened ricotta. Also delightful is a compote made with all the fruits the market has to offer: mix some raspberries, strawberries, pears, peaches and plums with tropical mangoes, kiwis, papayas, fresh dates and figs, pineapple and bananas. Over the compote strew some chopped walnuts, almonds or pistachios, and infuse the whole with a little white rum, Cognac, orange liqueur or amaretto.

Here are some sample menus for different occasions using recipes in this book. Naturally, they're just a jumping-off point.

When you'd like to bring back memories of Italy with family and friends:
Italian-Style Vegetables (page 20)
Saltimbocca alla Romana (page 76)
Zuppa Romana (page 113)
Both the first course and the dessert for this uncomplicated menu can be prepared ahead. The main dish takes so little time that you can spend the evening with your guests, not in the kitchen.

If you love unusual food combinations, here's an appealing collection:
Tomato Cream Soup (page 13)
Lamb Pilaf (page 78)
Tiramisù (page 112)
If it isn't tomato season, used canned tomatoes for the soup. The *tiramisù* is prepared the day before and refrigerated until serving time.

A simple meal that will satisfy the heartiest eaters:
Stuffed Peppers (page 84)
Tiramisù (page 112)
You can take your time preparing the main dish, because dessert is already made the day before.

A menu that's guaranteed to be a smashing success even for beginning cooks. A word of advice—buy crisp, bright green spinach and a young, fresh frying chicken:
Spinach with Pine Nuts (page 24)
Roast Chicken Stuffed with Scallion and Apple (page 58)
Crème Brûlée (page 107)
Prepare the *crème brûlée* the day before. To serve it you will simply have to sprinkle the custard with sugar and slip it under the broiler for a moment or two.

Another menu that will allow inexperienced cooks to dazzle their guests:
Spinach Gratin (page 24)
Tournedos in Morel Cream Sauce (page 40)
Chocolate Mousse (page 110)
The dessert can be made ahead.

This menu is light and summery. Serve it to guests who appreciate refined simplicity:
Tomato Cream Soup (page 13)
Marinated Lamb Chops (page 56)
Potato-Leek Gratin (page 94)
Tiramisù (page 112)
The dessert must be made a day ahead so it has time to ripen in the refrigerator. The vegetable-puree soup base can likewise be prepared the day before. Put the gratin in the oven when you serve cocktails or aperitifs; there will still be enough time to cook the lamb chops. Planned in this way the menu allows you plenty of time to mingle with your guests.

A thrifty dinner for cold winter evenings— but delicious enough for company:
Pichelstein One-Pot (page 14)
Steamed Hazelnut Pudding (page 108)
Cook both main dish and dessert at the same time; the pudding is good warm or cold, and you'll save time and energy.

This menu is a homage to French country cooking. It is easily accomplished even by inexperienced cooks:
Salade Niçoise (page 18)
Coq au Vin (page 60) with French bread
Fruit salad or assorted fresh fruits
Serve the first course when the chicken has about 15 minutes longer to cook. Dessert can be assembled ahead.

An autumnal feast for discriminating diners—but there's nothing difficult about the preparation.
Braised Oyster Mushrooms, half recipe (page 90)
Rabbit Stew with Prunes (page 66)
Spaetzle (page 96) or bread
Steamed Hazelnut Pudding (page 108)
This menu takes a bit of organization. Have all ingredients for the main dish and dessert prepared ahead of time, then stew the rabbit while the pudding steams.

A good summer menu for special occasions. It is not inexpensive, but you can rest assured that it will impress even the most finicky eaters:
Eggplant with Yogurt Cream (page 25)
Roast Leg of Lamb (page 54)
Green Beans with Bacon (page 86)
Swiss *Rösti* Potatoes (page 102), cooked in small portions.
Rote Grütze (page 109)
Except for the *Rote Grütze* this is not a do-ahead menu. Start roasting the lamb shortly before you serve the first course. Cook the *rösti* while lamb roasts and as it rests before carving.

For Christmas and other particularly festive occasions we're glad to spend a little extra for an exceptional meal. This menu also requires more time than most, but it more than repays the effort:
Marrow Ball Soup (page 10)
Rare Filet of Venison (page 64)
Spaetzle (page 96) and red cabbage
Charlotte Royale (page 114)
The venison sauce base can be made several days in advance (or well in advance and frozen); likewise the soup broth.

An easy summer menu with which you can serve a goodly group of people:
Greek Farmer's Salad (page 18)
Roast Beef with Sauce Béarnaise (page 42), accompanied by baked potatoes, French or Italian bread
Real Vanilla Bavarian Cream (page 104)
Serve the Greek salad while the roast beef is resting in foil. The dessert can be prepared ahead of time.

For a change of pace, offer your guests a Far Eastern entree paired with a dessert straight out of classic French cuisine:
Sweet and Sour Pork (page 80) with steamed rice
Crème Brûlée (page 107)
Though the pork must be cooked at the last minute, this should pose no particular problems since the rice can be kept warm in the oven and the dessert will be waiting in the refrigerator, needing just a moment's attention for its final glaze.

Serve this menu on a happy occasion, or perhaps just for Sunday dinner when you want to pamper the family with something special:
Spinach with Pine Nuts (page 24)
Pork Tenderloin in Puff Pastry (page 32)
Real Vanilla Bavarian Cream (page 104)
The dessert can be readied in advance and the assembled, pastry-wrapped tenderloin can be prepared up to two hours ahead and refrigerated—in fact, this will make the pastry especially light and flaky.

A deliciously light meal that's best in summer, when fresh, fully ripened fruits and vegetables are at their peak:
Salade Niçoise (page 18)
Foil-Baked Fish (page 29)
French or Italian bread
Rote Grütze (page 109)

When the family finances are feeling a pinch, give this menu a try. Even the resident epicures will be delighted:
Tomato Cream Soup (page 13)
Frikadellen (page 52)
Piquant Potato Salad (page 98)
Rote Grütze (page 109)
The *Rote Grütze* can be made with frozen berries.

An impressive menu that will pose no problems for the cook, this is suitable for a casual gathering of close friends or for more formal dinners:
Italian-Style Vegetables (page 20)
Beef Stroganoff (page 48) with
Spaetzle (page 96) or rice
Chocolate Mousse (page 110)
The first course and dessert can be made in advance. When you're serving *spaetzle* as a side dish, cook them a bit ahead of time, toss them with butter and keep hot in the oven.

Satisfying classics for those who appreciate the finest. Serve this when entertaining a smallish group:

Marrow Ball Soup (page 10)
Boiled Beef with Chive Sauce (page 46)
Raw-Potato Home Fries (page 103)
Griessflammeri (page 106)
For the soup, use broth left from the main dish. Remember to leave plenty of time for the meat to cook, and to prepare the dessert a day ahead so that it will be thoroughly chilled and will unmold easily.

The main course and dessert here are so hearty and satisfying that we've skipped the appetizer:
Half-and-Half Goulash (page 36)
Spaetzle (page 96)
Griessflammeri (page 106)
Except for the *spaetzle*, this is strictly do-ahead; in fact, the goulash can be made far in advance, for it freezes superbly. The *Griessflammeri* should be made the day before serving.

A thrifty Sunday supper, given a special accent by the oyster mushrooms:
Potato Soup with Bacon, half recipe (page 12)
Stuffed Meat Loaf (page 53)
Braised Oyster Mushrooms (page 90) with boiled potatoes
Fresh fruit

For those who love high-quality but unpretentious home cooking:
Marrow Ball Soup (page 10)
Crusty Roast Pork (page 30)
Raw-Potato Dumplings (page 101) with red cabbage
Rote Grütze (page 109)
The soup broth can be prepared ahead; so can the marrow balls, which can also be frozen. If you're in a hurry, make the dumplings from one of the imported mixes available in European delis. The *Rote Grütze* should be made in advance so that it will be well chilled.

Index

Conversion Tables

The following are conversion tables and other information applicable to those converting the recipes in this book for use in other English-speaking countries. The cup and spoon measures given in this book are U.S. Customary (1 cup = 236 mL; 1 tablespoon = 15 mL). Use these tables when working with British Imperial or Metric kitchen utensils.

Liquid Measures

The Imperial pint is larger than the U.S. pint; therefore note the following when measuring liquid ingredients.

U.S.

1 cup = 8 fluid ounces
½ cup = 4 fluid ounces
1 tablespoon = ¾ fluid ounce

IMPERIAL

1 cup = 10 fluid ounces
½ cup = 5 fluid ounces
1 tablespoon = 1 fluid ounce

U.S. MEASURE	METRIC*	IMPERIAL*
1 quart (4 cups)	950 mL	1½ pints + 4 tablespoons
1 pint (2 cups)	450 mL	¾ pint
1 cup	236 mL	¼ pint + 6 tablespoons
1 tablespoon	15 mL	1+ tablespoon
1 teaspoon	5 mL	1 teaspoon

*Note that exact quantities cannot always be given. Differences are more crucial when dealing with larger quantities. For teaspoon and tablespoon measures, simply use scant quantities, or for more accurate conversions rely upon metric measures.

Solid Measures

Outside the U.S., cooks measure more items by weight. Here are approximate equivalents for basic items in this book.*

	U.S. CUSTOMARY	METRIC	IMPERIAL
Apples (peeled and chopped)	2 cups	225 g	8 ounces
Beans (dried, raw)	1 cup	225 g	8 ounces
Butter	1 cup	225 g	8 ounces
	½ cup	115 g	4 ounces
	¼ cup	60 g	2 ounces
	1 tablespoon	15 g	½ ounce
Cheese (grated)	1 cup	115 g	4 ounces
Chocolate chips	½ cup	85 g	3 ounces
Coconut (shredded)	½ cup	60 g	2 ounces
Fruit (chopped)	1 cup	225 g	8 ounces
Herbs (chopped)	¼ cup	7 g	¼ ounce

	U.S. CUSTOMARY	METRIC	IMPERIAL
Meats/Chicken (chopped, cooked)	1 cup	175 g	6 ounces
Mushrooms (chopped)	1 cup	70 g	2½ ounces
Nut Meats (chopped)	1 cup	115 g	4 ounces
Pasta (dried; raw)	1 cup	225 g	8 ounces
Peas (shelled)	1 cup	225 g	8 ounces
Potatoes (mashed)	2 cups	450 g	1 pound
Raisins (and other dried fruits)	1 cup	175 g	6 ounces
Rice (uncooked)	1 cup	225 g	8 ounces
(cooked)	3 cups	225 g	8 ounces
Spinach (cooked)	½ cup	285 g	10 ounces
Vegetables (chopped, raw: onions, celery)	1 cup	115 g	4 ounces

*So as to avoid awkward measurements, some conversions are not exact.

Dry Measures

The following items are measured by weight outside of the U.S. These items are variable, especially the flour, depending on individual variety of flour and moisture. American cup measurements on the following items are loosely packed; flour is measured directly from package (presifted).

	U.S. CUSTOMARY	METRIC	IMPERIAL
Flour (all-purpose or plain)	1 cup	150 g	5 ounces
(bread or strong)	½ cup	70 g	2½ ounces
(cake)	1 cup	125 g	4¼ ounces
Cornmeal	1 cup	175 g	6 ounces
Bran	1 cup	60 g	2 ounces
Wheat Germ	1 cup	85 g	3 ounces
Rolled Oats (raw)	1 cup	115 g	4 ounces
Sugar (granulated or caster)	1 cup	190 g	6½ ounces
	½ cup	85 g	3 ounces
	¼ cup	40 g	1¾ ounces
(confectioners or icing)	1 cup	80 g	2⅔ ounces
	½ cup	40 g	1⅓ ounces
	¼ cup	20 g	¾ ounce
(soft brown)	1 cup	160 g	5⅓ ounces
	½ cup	80 g	2⅔ ounces
	¼ cup	40 g	1⅓ ounces

Oven Temperatures

Gas Mark	¼	2	4	6	8
Fahrenheit	225	300	350	400	450
Celsius	110	150	180	200	230

C.P. Fischer
A food photographer with his own test kitchen, C.P. Fischer photographed all the recipes in this book. International public relations firms and the food industry are numbered among his clients. Many of his books have received awards from the German Gastronomic Academy.

Mechthild Piepenbrock
A food scientist with many publications to her credit, Mechthild Piepenbrock has been a freelance food journalist and cookbook author for many years. Several of her books have been honored by the German Gastronomic Academy.

Barbara Rias-Bucher
A native of Munich, Ms. Rias-Bucher has collaborated on and edited cookbooks for a Munich publisher. She has written her own series of cookbooks, and the subject of cooking has occupied her ever since her youth —first as a hobby, then professionally. Since 1979 she has worked as a freelance food journalist.